THE SELECTED POEMS
OF TU FU

Writing

Awakened Cosmos:
   The Mind of Classical Chinese Poetry (*Essay*)
Desert (*Poetry*)
The Wilds of Poetry:
   Adventures in Mind and Landscape (*Essay*)
Existence: A Story (*Essay*)
Hunger Mountain:
   A Field Guide to Mind and Landscape (*Essay*)
Fossil Sky (*Poetry*)

Translation

No-Gate Gateway
I Ching: The Book of Change
The Late Poems of Wang An-shih
The Four Chinese Classics
Classical Chinese Poetry: An Anthology
The Selected Poems of Wang Wei
The Mountain Poems of Meng Hao-jan
Mountain Home: The Wilderness Poetry of Ancient China
The Mountain Poems of Hsieh Ling-yün
Tao Te Ching
The Selected Poems of Po Chü-i
The Analects
Mencius
Chuang Tzu: The Inner Chapters
The Late Poems of Meng Chiao
The Selected Poems of Li Po
The Selected Poems of T'ao Ch'ien
The Selected Poems of Tu Fu

THE SELECTED POEMS
OF TU FU

Expanded and Newly Translated by

David Hinton

A NEW DIRECTIONS PAPERBOOK ORIGINAL

Manufactured in the United States of America
First published as a New Directions Paperbook (NDP1470) in 2020
Book design by Eileen Bellamy

Library of Congress Cataloging-in-Publication Data
Names: Du, Fu, 712–770, author. | Hinton, David, 1954– translator.
Title: The selected poems of Tu Fu / Tu Fu ; expanded and newly translated by David Hinton.
Description: First New Directions edition. | New York : New Directions Publishing, [2019]
Identifiers: LCCN 2019047021 | ISBN 9780811228381 (paperback) | ISBN 9780811224062 (ebook)
Subjects: LCSH: Du, Fu, 712–770—Translations into English.
Classification: LCC PL2675 .A2 2019 | DDC 895.11/3—dc23
LC record available at https://lccn.loc.gov/2019047021

10 9 8 7 6 5 4

New Directions Books are published for James Laughlin
by New Directions Publishing Corporation
80 Eighth Avenue, New York 10011

ndbooks.com

CONTENTS

THE SELECTED POEMS
OF TU FU

INTRODUCTION

THE CHINESE POETIC tradition is the largest and longest contin-
uous tradition in world literature—practiced by virtually everyone
in the educated class, and stretching from somewhere deep in the
oral tradition (translations of which are the beginning of the written tradi-
tion) to the present, migrating along the way to Korea and Japan, where it
was adopted and transformed into their own, and more recently to modern
America, where its terms of practice defined the fundamental operating as-
sumptions of twentieth-century poetry. Among the countless poets in the
ancient Chinese tradition, Tu Fu (712–770 CE) is generally acknowledged
to be the greatest. In its sweep and intensity, his life feels beyond all human
scale, most notably his last decade, during which the country was ravaged by
civil war. He spent those years as a refugee from his devastated homeland in
the north, wandering the western and southern borders of Chinese cultural
influence, struggling against poverty and dislocation and often fleeing local
outbreaks of fighting. It was an existence that would have silenced any nor-
mal poet, but Tu somehow wrote steadily through it all. In fact, he wrote
the vast majority of his poems during that final decade.

The reasons usually given for Tu Fu's stature sound recognizable
enough in terms of Western poetry: virtuosic wisdom and insight in poem
after poem. A poetic engagement with the full range of human experi-
ence—the everyday and routine, the unsavory and "unpoetic," private spir-
itual cultivation and philosophical exploration, public poems about social
injustice and the horrors of war—a range that was often combined into
single poems and that created new complexities and depths of experience,
most notably perhaps the black late poems of existential exposure that cast
the human against the elemental sweep of the universe. Tu masterfully used

and transformed every poetic form imaginable in his time: concise imagistic poems with only four lines; a more-developed eight-line form capable of expanded imagistic and philosophic depths; sprawling narratives; interconnected lyric sequences that create a new layering of complexity. As far as these terms are concerned, the poems in translation speak for themselves. But the philosophical assumptions shaping Chinese poetry invest Tu's poetic work with deeper dimensions that aren't apparent in translation.

Poetry in ancient China was a form of spiritual practice; and as spiritual practice in China was always about self-cultivation, it makes sense that poetry was also considered a window onto the deepest levels of a poet's mind. Poetry was the embodiment and measure of a poet's deep wisdom, and it is here that Tu Fu's greatness is most profoundly revealed in his mastery of ancient China's Taoist and Ch'an (Zen) Buddhist insight. Or more precisely, the ways his poems enact Taoist/Ch'an insight as immediate experience for the reader.

The Taoist/Ch'an philosophical framework began with Lao Tzu's\ *Tao Te Ching* (c. sixth century BCE)—a seminal work of Taoism, the spiritual root of Chinese philosophy. Lao Tzu's central concern was *Tao*, which originally meant "way," as in a road or pathway. But Lao Tzu used it to describe the empirical Cosmos as a single living tissue that is inexplicably generative—and so female in its very nature. As such, it is an ongoing cosmological process, an ontological path*Way* by which things emerge from that generative tissue as distinct forms, evolve through their lives, and then vanish back into that tissue, only to be transformed and reemerge in new forms.

The abiding aspiration of spiritual and poetic practice in ancient China was to dwell at the deepest levels as an organic part of Tao's generative cosmological process—to cultivate consciousness as belonging to this larger whole, and to understand that larger whole as one's truest self. The cultivation of this dwelling also defined Ch'an Buddhist practice. Ch'an originated in the fourth century CE through an amalgamation of Taoism and recently imported Buddhism, and was thereafter widely considered by artist-intellectuals as a form of Taoist thought refined and reconfigured by Buddhist meditation practice. Tu Fu apparently received extensive Ch'an training in his youth, years during which he apparently mastered the two fundamental dimensions of Ch'an practice, and those dimensions came to define the deep structure for his poetry (as it did for virtually all Chinese poetry, as well as painting and calligraphy).

The first dimension of Ch'an practice is meditation, which was a widespread practice among ancient China's artist-intellectuals. In its barest outlines, meditation involved sitting quietly and watching thoughts come and go in a field of emptiness. From this attention to thought's movement came meditation's first revelation: that we are, as a matter of observable fact, separate from our thoughts and memories, choices and judgments. That is, we are not the center of identity we assume ourselves to be in our day-to-day lives—that center of self-absorbed thought that takes reality (Tao's cosmological tissue) as the object of its contemplation, defining us as fundamentally outside reality. Instead, we are the empty awareness (known in Ch'an terminology as "empty-mind") that watches identity rehearsing itself in thoughts and memories, choices and judgments, all relentlessly coming and going.

With experience, the thought process slowed, and it was possible for adepts like Tu Fu to watch thoughts burgeon forth out of the dark emptiness, evolve through their transformations, and disappear back into it. The revelation here was that thoughts appear and disappear in exactly the same way as the ten thousand things appear and disappear in the process of Tao's unfurling. From this comes the realization that thought and the things of this world are therefore both part of the same tissue: hence, no fundamental distinction between the processes of mind and Cosmos.

Eventually the stream of thought fell silent, and adepts inhabited empty-mind, that generative ground itself. Here, they were wholly free of the center of identity—free, that is, of the self-absorbed and relentless process of thought that defines us as centers of identity separate from the world around us. This was the heart of dwelling in ancient China: consciousness and Cosmos woven together in the most profound cosmological and ontological way, identity revealed in its most primal form as the generative tissue itself.

Once the mind was silent, perception became a spiritual practice: the opening of consciousness become a bottomless mirror allowing no distinction between inside and outside, consciousness again integral to empirical reality. Or put another way, it is the material Cosmos awakened to itself, open to itself. This mirroring is the very fabric of Chinese poetry, manifest in its texture of imagistic clarity. And such imagery resounds in another way, for the things of this world are all details of Tao's perpetual unfolding according to its own nature. To simply record them in a poem is to allow them to exist as much as possible in their sheer thusness, free of our human constructions.

And so, in simply recording facts in this way, a poet dwells as part of that unfolding—dwells, in fact, at the perpetual origin of that unfolding.

Normally in Chinese poetry, this imagistic practice involves rivers-and-mountains landscape, where Tao's unfolding is most majestically and immediately visible, and there is no lack of rivers and mountains in Tu Fu's work. He sometimes even describes that mirroring as landscape practice directly: "In a river's clarity, you can polish mind jewel-bright." And taking this a step further, in a poem written at a Ch'an mountain monastery (p. 134), he says: "I turn / and gaze into mind that dwells nowhere."

But rather than limiting Ch'an imagery to landscape, Tu included all aspects of experience: from the everyday and the unpoetic to the ravages of war. It is what we might call a rigorous realism, and in the Taoist/Ch'an framework, that realism is almost synonymous with enlightenment: consciousness as the awakened Cosmos open equally to creation and destruction, beauty and terror, joy and grief. Open to it all and open to feeling itself in every possible way. And Tu's images operated at an unprecedented level of detail. So in his imagistic practice, Tu expanded Ch'an insight across the full range of human experience. And that is a large part of Tu Fu's greatness within the Chinese tradition.

While meditation is quiet and self-effacing, the second dimension of Taoist/Ch'an self-cultivation is quite the opposite: wild and self-projecting. This practice was known as *wu-wei*, meaning "not acting" in the sense of acting without the metaphysics of self, or of being absent when you act. This selfless action is the movement of Tao itself, so *wu-wei* practice cultivates action as integral to Tao's spontaneous process, which ancient artist-intellectuals recognized most dramatically in rivers-and-mountains landscapes. To practice *wu-wei* is to move with the wild energy of the Cosmos itself, and Tu Fu's poetic practice reveals him as a master of *wu-wei* in a number of ways.

Tu wrote openly and effortlessly about all aspects of experience—whatever he happened to encounter, no matter how mundane. Here, Tu's *wu-wei* practice is an extension of his Ch'an realism, and it is perhaps most remarkable in the way that he wrote steadily through all the debilitating challenges of his day-to-day refugee life. And this practice went so far as to include a great many poems that simply traced a fleeting moment of thought, accepting and valuing it even though it had no real "poetic interest" in any conventional sense. As for the poems themselves: they tend to follow the movement of his thought, giving them a spontaneous associative texture. In shorter poems, this creates a subtle sense of collage made up of striking juxtapositions (this becomes more prominent in later poems). And his longer poems tend to move in a kind of liberated ramble following the transformations of experience and thought. Choices and judgments are part of what define us as identity-centers separate from the world, but Tu's poetic practice accepted all aspects of experience and any movement of thought equally: self integral to Cosmos, to Tao's process unfolding without choice or judgment.

Tu Fu rarely talks about these philosophical issues explicitly, though they do come up. He is generally described as a social poet who had little interest in Taoist/Ch'an cultivation. But even when the poems are political, and many are, they are shaped at a deep level by Taoist/Ch'an assumptions. Indeed, his mastery of Taoist/Ch'an insight is the very form of his poetry and his life. And this is exactly why Tu inspired such awe among other poets and artist-intellectuals: the sense that he was always already enlightened, his poetry rarely cultivating spiritual insight explicitly as so many other major poets did. And rather than an enlightenment in the protected environs of a monastic or recluse life, Tu's operated out in a deeply compromised world of historical urgency (he was called the "poet-historian"), expanding Taoist/Ch'an insight across a new breadth of personal experience. Masterfully combining imagistic clarity with *wu-wei* movement, Tu was nothing less than the Cosmos awakened to itself, thinking and feeling itself in the particular form of a poet who lived for a few decades in T'ang Dynasty China.

READING GUIDE

T HE CONCEPTUAL FRAMEWORK sketched in the introduction is described in more depth and detail in the *Key Terms* section at the back of the book, which defines a constellation of essential philosophical concepts. This section can be read piecemeal, as the concepts are encountered in the poems (notes reference *Key Terms*), or it can be read as a whole.

That conceptual framework is described still more extensively in a companion volume, *Awakened Cosmos: The Mind of Classical Chinese Poetry*, which discusses at length nineteen of the poems translated in this book. The essays in *Awakened Cosmos* focus on specific and detailed ways that the Taoist/Ch'an conceptual framework operates in the original poems. They attempt to open dimensions of the poems that are untranslatable, primarily because of the very different nature of the classical Chinese language and the Taoist/Ch'an conceptual framework. In this, they reveal deeper levels of the wisdom China's artist-intellectuals so admired in Tu Fu, and how that wisdom shaped the broad range of experience manifest in Tu's dramatic life. At the same time, the essays offer another way into the deep levels of the Taoist/Ch'an conceptual framework, for rendering Taoist/Ch'an insight as lived experience was the foundation of poetic practice in Tu Fu's China.

TU FU'S CHINA

NORTH: EARLY POEMS

(737–755)

ORN IN 712, Tu Fu lived until middle age during the High T'ang Dynasty, one of Chinese civilization's great moments in terms of both cultural achievement and social well-being. In a time when the vast majority of the population was illiterate, Tu's family belonged to the elite aristocracy, the literate class that ran the government and produced the national culture. His father came from a long line of respected scholar-officials. His mother was a great granddaughter of the emperor who founded the T'ang Dynasty. This heritage gave Tu widespread and prominent connections, and in his life of poverty and refugee wandering, he would often depend upon their generosity. Tu's mother died soon after he was born. His father remarried, and this marriage added three stepbrothers and one stepsister to the family.

Much of Tu's youth was spent traveling without his family. Such travels were highly unusual, but for Tu they included long stays in the capital, Peace-Perpetua (Ch'ang-an, today's Xian), and in many locations throughout China, making him remarkably cosmopolitan. During those years he also received a rigorous classical education and apparently quite extensive Ch'an (Zen) Buddhist training, much of it no doubt in monasteries where he stayed during his travels.

Any young man from Tu Fu's class aspired to become a government official. Not only were the practical advantages considerable (intellectual/ artistic opportunity and companionship, wealth, prestige), but in the Confucian order, helping the emperor care for the people was a scholar's only proper place. Tu was brilliant and one of the elite candidates from the capital region, but he somehow failed the qualifying exam for governmental positions when he was twenty-four, and his nomadic life continued until 752, his fortieth year. Then, because Tu's abilities had impressed so many people over the years, the emperor finally ordered a special examination for him, and he passed.

Tu waited several years for a position, living at the capital and his ancestral village in the mountains just south of there. By then he was over forty and married to a woman who was some twenty years younger. A son was born in the village, and over the next four years, Tu's wife gave birth to two daughters and two more sons. One of these sons died in 755 (p. 35), however, leaving the couple with two daughters and two sons for most of their married life. (Another daughter was born in 767, but she died one year later.)

Tu Fu, who has been honored as a devoted father and husband, now began a desperate struggle to support his wife and children, a struggle that would continue throughout most of his life. Tu's lifelong health problems also began at this time, when he developed chronic asthma. Finally he moved the family to First-Devotion, a village north of the capital where he apparently had some means of support, then returned to the capital. When he *eventually* obtained a position as advisor to the crown prince, Tu returned to First-Devotion to retrieve his family (p. 33).

Gazing at the Sacred Peak

What is this ancestor Exalt Mountain like?
Endless greens of north and south meeting

where Changemaker distills divine beauty,
where *yin* and *yang* cleave dusk and dawn.

Chest heaving breathes out cloud, and eyes
open dusk bird-flight home. One day soon,

on the summit, peaks ranging away will be
small enough to hold, all in a single glance.

Wandering at Dragon-Gate's
Ancestor-Devotion Monastery

At four-directions monastery, I wander off,
stay the night in four-directions borderland.

Born of the valley's *yin*-dark, empty music
drifts, moon-forest pellucid shadow-scatters.

Heaven-rift planets and stars gathered close
here—I sleep all cloud-mist and chill robes,

then beginning to stir, hear the morning bell
call out, opening such depths of awakening.

Inscribed on a Wall at Longbow's Recluse Home

Amid spring mountains, alone, I set out to find you.
Axe strokes *crack—crack*, and quit. Quiet mystery

deepens. I follow a stream up into last snow and ice
and beyond, dusk light aslant, to Stone Gate forests.

Deer roam all morning here, for you harm nothing.
Wanting nothing, you know *ch'i* gold and silver all

night. Facing you *on a whim* in such dark, the way
home lost—I feel it drifting, this whole empty boat.

Dinner with Two Friends at Stone-Gate Mountain

The clarity of autumn water is bottomless,
a breezy serenity rinsing our minds clean.

One friend wanders lazily away *on a whim*,
the other sets out on horseback to find him.

A mere clerk, I meet this precious-jade pair,
and get a splendid meal for one single coin,

then dusk comes: flute song adrift, perfect.
And from river deeps, dragons too sing out.

Thoughts, Facing Rain: I Go to Invite a Guest In

Exalt Mountain clouds and peaks billow up,
surge to swell, fill the vast emptiness where

all things begin. Thunder on painted screens
startles swallows. Wild rains drive fish deep.

Sitting here facing cheap sage-wisdom wine,
I hear your carriage outside. Helpless against

miserable mud, I go to invite you in, calling
Bring your horse right up to the porch steps.

War-Cart Chant

War-carts clatter and creak,
horses stomp and splutter:
each wearing quiver and bow, the war-bound men pass.

Mothers and fathers, wives and children—they all flock
alongside, farewell dust so thick you can't see All-Solar,

grief's bridge. They get everywhere in the way, crying
cries to break against heaven, tugging at war clothes.

On the roadside, when a passerby asks war-bound men,
war-bound men say simply: *Our lots are so often drawn.*

Taken north at fifteen, we guard Yellow River shorelines,
and taken west at forty, we man frontier battle camps.

Village elders tied our head-cloths then. And here we
return, hair white, only to leave again for borderlands,

lands swollen with seas of blood. And our fine emperor's
imperial dreams of conquest never end, they never end.

Has no one heard that
east of mountains, in our homeland, ten hundred towns
and ten thousand villages are overrun by thorned weeds,

that even though strong wives keep hoeing and plowing,
you can't tell where crops are and aren't? It's worst for

Thresh-Grain warriors: the more bitter war they outlive,
the more they're herded around like chickens and dogs.

Though you're kind to ask, sir,
how could we complain? Imagine

this winter in Thresh-Grain: men
still haven't returned, and those

clerks are out demanding taxes.
Taxes! How can people pay taxes?

A son's birth means tragedy now.
People prefer a daughter's birth,

a daughter's birth might at least end in marriage nearby,
but a son's birth ends in an open grave who knows where.

Has no one seen
how bones from ancient times
lie, bleached and unclaimed, scattered along shores of

Sky-Blue Seas—how the bitter weeping of old ghosts is
joined by new voices, the gray sky by chittering rain.

Onward Across Borders

I

So far from my village, O sent so far
away into deep Weave River country.

Reporting dates are final. Anyone who
resists gets tangled in nets of calamity.

Our emperor's lands rich enough and
more: What good's a few extra acres?

Shouldering a spear, lost, my parents'
love lost, I choke down silence and go.

2

I left home long ago, walked out our gate
into the unbearable abuse soldiers endure.

Bones of father's love, flesh of mother's:
how are they so broken in a son still alive

to guess at death: shaking free of its reins,
the horse tearing blue silk from my hands,

or scrambling eighty thousand feet down
mountain slopes, reaching for a fallen flag.

3

I sharpen my sword in a river of hushed
cries, river bleeding as the edge cuts my

hand open. Longing to ease heart-slash
cries turns the mind to thread-ends ever

tangled. And once dedicated to country,
what could a good man resent? Heroes'

portraits hang in Dragon-Horse Temple,
and bones of war crumble quickly away.

4

Always some elder to scare-up men,
keep distant frontiers well-supplied.

Death certain as life, we advance—
but still, officers keep raging at us.

Meeting a friend on the road, I send
letters home. O how are we broken

so far apart, so far we'll never even
scrape-by in sorrow together again?

5

Distant, ten thousand miles and more
distant, they sent us to fill vast armies,

armies full of strange joys and griefs.
How could generals hear everything?

Riders appear across the river, sudden
and fast, ten hundred Mongol brigades.

From this slave's beginning, how long
until my honor's made and confirmed?

6

If you draw a bow, draw the strongest.
If you shoot arrows, shoot the longest.

Shooting men, first shoot their horses.
Seizing enemies, first seize their chief.

But killing must be kept within limits.
A country is nothing without borders,

and if there's any hope of ending these
invasions, it isn't slaughter and death.

7

Pushing our horses hard through sleet-
smeared sky, we enter high mountains

and the trail gets risky. Fingers digging
through layers of ice, we hug cold rock,

so far from our Chinese moon. O when
will we ever go back to tend city-walls?

Clouds drift away south at dusk, clouds
I can watch but never ride home, home.

8

The Mongols try an assault on our walls,
and for hundreds of miles, dust-choked

wind darkens skies. A few brave sword-
strokes send their army scattering away,

and we capture a famed chieftain, return
to present him hog-tied at the main gate.

Soon we're herded back into formation,
ready to march. One win, so much talk.

9

In ten warrior years and more, how
could I avoid all honor? Everyone

treasures heroes, but how shameful
to talk myself up like all the others.

War smolders across our heartland
and rages on the frontiers: all those

lords chasing ambition everywhere,
who can elude *resolute in privation*?

New Year's Eve

Songs over pepper wine have ended.
Friends jubilant among friends, we

start a stable racket of horses. Wind-
lamps blaze, scattering forest crows.

Dawn, the fortieth year of my flight
into dusk light's over. Who changes,

who even slows this dead dazzling
drunk in the wings of life we live?

A Friend Stops By on a Summer Day

In distant forests, summer heat easing,
you happen by in your wandering. It's

like some wildland village: my simple
house just inside the city's south wall,

neighbors open and so simple-hearted,
needs easily filled. Call next door, ask

neighbors on the west if they can spare
any wine, and suddenly a jarful comes

across the fence—fresh, unfiltered. We
open mats beside Meandering River's

long currents, crystalline winds arrive,
and you're startled it's already autumn.

Birds nest everywhere, bicker and cry,
tightening cicada song fills lush leaves:

in this wild racket of things, who could
say this thatch-hut is quiet in mystery?

We linger out flawless blossoms dusk-
tinted on water—a world enough now,

enough. And the winejar far from empty,
I set out with schemes aplenty for more.

9/9 Festival: Sent to Summit-Now

I step outside for a moment, then back in.
It's the same foundering clouds and rain,

mud-choked water sloshing everywhere.
Growing thin with worry about you, I sit

on a west porch muttering hushed chants.
Nights and days blur together, meals too,

and though Meandering River's mere steps
away, how could we ever meet there now?

How much, O how much must our simple
people endure? Their farms are past hope,

and if we scold the god of cloud and rain,
who'll patch these leak-ravaged heavens?

Sun and moon lost to a radiant haze and
waste world—creatures twitter and howl,

as the noble-minded take to twisted paths
and common folk run themselves ragged.

Even that exalted South Mountain might
already have sunk into floods and drifted

away. What is it for, here at my east fence,
this festive confusion of chrysanthemums?

All those fine new poems you're writing?
Our shared weakness for wine? Cut them,

I'll cut those yellow-cheer things, fill my
sleeves far too beautiful for nothing today.

Autumn Rain Lament

Foundering rain, reckless wind: an indiscriminate ruins of
autumn. Four seas and eight horizons, the whole world all

one cloud—you can't tell horses going from oxen coming,
or muddy Deep-Flow River from crystal-clear Moon-Field.

Wheat-seed sprouts ears in the field, millet seed rots black:
who knows what farm families are doing? Here in the city,

people barter quilts for a few handfuls of rice. These days,
folks take what they can get. No one mentions old bargains.

First-Devotion Return Chant

.   .   .

The hundred grasses in tatters, high wind-
scoured ridges and stars—it is year's end

on the imperial highway. Mountain dark
towering into the heart of night, I set out.

Soon I can't tie my loose coat-sash closed,
fingers frostbitten among bitter morning

peaks. Our emperor's sound asleep there
on Black-Horse Mountain, demon banners

trailed skyward in this icy canyon passing
armies polished smooth. Steam billowing

over his jasper-green pools, constellations
chafe and jar against his imperial lances.

Regal ministers were up late taking their
fine pleasure here. Music swelling through

gnarled canyons, not a poor man in sight,
they were bathed by their choice women,

women pampered with silks painstakingly
woven out by shivering farm wives, their

husbands horsewhipped by tax collectors
come demanding tributes for that palace.

And our sage emperor, wishing people well,
sends baskets stuffed with heartfelt gifts?

With trusted ministers this blind to inner-
pattern, why squander all those supplies?

The number of august men dawn brings
to court frightens decent folk. And I hear

the emperor's own gold tableware's been
divvied-out among blue-blooded families.

Dancing goddesses grace halls, jade-pure
bodies furling incense mists. And grieving

flutes echoing a *ch'in* song's purest clarity,
furs warm, guests savor camel-hoof soup,

frost-whipped kumquats and fragrant coolie
oranges. The grand imperial-red gate: rank

wine and meat dumped inside, dead bones
frozen by the road outside. All and nothing

here but a key and half-step different. How
could such misery endured ever be retold?

I turn north to Deep-Flow and Moon-Field
rivers. And at a flooded ferry, I turn again.

A sea of water pouring from the west looms
and summits to the end of sight and beyond

to Empty-Alike Mountain peaks, and I fear
it may wreck the pillars holding up heaven.

One bridge still spans the river, its welcome
trestlework a creaking howl and whisper in

high wind, and we travelers help each other
across the current raging broad and frenzied.

My dear wife in a strange place, sheltering
our family from wind and snow: why did I

leave them so long alone? Thinking we'll
at least all be together again going without,

I come home to sounds of weeping, wailing
cries for a child stone-dead now of hunger.

Neighbors sob in the street. And who am I
to master my grief like some sage, ashamed

even to be a father—I whose son has died
for simple lack of food? After full autumn

harvests, how could I have suspected, how
imagined the poor so desperate with want?

Son of an untaxed family, not dragged off
to make someone's war, I have lived a life

charmed, and still too sad. O but the poor
grieve like vast wind across ravaged trees:

those who've lost all for war, those on far
frontiers dead, they wander dark thoughts,

and elusive engines of grief still loom like
all South Mountain, heave and swing loose.

NORTH: CIVIL WAR

(755–759)

BEFORE TU FU could move his family back to the capital, his long-awaited success fell victim to the major political event of his time: a devastating civil war. It was 755, Tu Fu's forty-third year, and the T'ang Dynasty never fully recovered from the war and the chronic militarism that it spawned. The fall in census figures from fifty-three million before the fighting to only seventeen million afterward summarizes the war's catastrophic impact: thirty-six million people were left either dead or displaced and homeless.

Rebel armies quickly conquered the capital, driving the government into exile at Phoenix-Soar to the west. The emperor, in his grief, abdicated to his son. And as Tu had recently been appointed advisor to that son, he was now an advisor to the emperor. Tu took his family still further north (p. 45) to the town of Deer-Altar, where he hoped they would be safe; then he set out to join the exile court. But for reasons unknown, he ended up in the occupied capital, where he was trapped for a year (pp. 39–44), hiding his identity from the rebel armies in part by living in a Ch'an monastery. He apparently contracted malaria during this year, an illness that would recur for the rest of his life.

Eventually, Tu Fu escaped and made his way to the exile court, where he took up his post as advisor to the new emperor. He thought his family had been overrun by war—but after a year without news, he heard they were safe and quickly set out on another difficult journey (p. 48) to rejoin them. Soon thereafter, loyal armies retook the capital, and Tu returned there with the court. His family soon joined him in the capital, where he was optimistic and working diligently as the emperor's advisor. But this happy situation hardly lasted more than six months: because of his association with a group that had fallen out of favor with the emperor, he was transferred to a position in a town east of the capital—a mild form of exile.

Array-Delight Lament

Early winter across ten prefectures, noble homes: their children
bleed now into Array-Delight, blood making water in the marsh.

Night open wide, skies crystalline depths, the battle gone silent:
leaving forty thousand loyal warriors dead there in a single day,

Mongols come thronging back, their arrows bathed blood-black,
and out drunk in the markets again, they mangle Mongol songs.

We of the capital—we turn away, face north to mourn and gaze
and, another day gone dark, long for our army's sudden return.

Moonlit Night

Tonight at Deer-Altar, she watches this very
moon alone at home. And those little, far-off

kids, too young to understand what keeps me
away, or even remember the capital. By now

her hair will be mist-scented, her jade-pure
arms chilled in its crystalline light. O when

will it find us together, drapes drawn empty
open, light traced where it's dried our tears?

Facing Snow

Enough new ghosts to mourn any war,
and a lone old grief-sung man. Broken

clouds at twilight's ragged edge, wind
buffets a dance of frenzied snow. Ladle

beside my jar drained of emerald wine,
flame-red illusion lingers in the stove.

News comes from nowhere. I sit spirit-
wounded, trace words empty onto sky.

Spring Landscape

The country in ruins, rivers and mountains
continue. The city grows lush with spring.

Blossoms scatter tears for us, and all these
separations in a bird's cry startle the heart.

Beacon-fires three months ablaze: by now
a mere letter's worth ten thousand in gold,

and worry's thinned my hair to such white
confusion I can't even keep this hairpin in.

Thinking of My Little Boy

We're apart still, and already oriole song
fills warm spring days. Changing seasons

startle me in all this separation, my little
sage, and who talks philosophy with you

there? Creeks and paths, empty mountains,
brushwood gate, a village of ancient trees:

for longing, there's always sleep. Sunning
on the porch, I nod off beneath blue skies.

Master Illumine's Rooms, Great-Cloud Monastery

Lamps blot and flare. Sleepless, I breathe
delicate mystery of incense, mind clarity

itself. The meditation hall stands proud in
depths of night. Gold windchimes clitter.

Spring courtyards sunk in heaven's dark,
earth's clarity insists on its hidden scents,

Jade-String stars shimmer, broken where
rooftop phoenix-metal wheels and soars.

We step out into Buddha-dawn half-light,
then back as bells fade. Morning's bright

awakening: in these fertile lands, it's grief
over the dust-and-sand onslaught of it all.

Ample-Flag Chant

I won't forget long ago slipping away
into precarious depths of night. Moon-

light radiant on White-River Mountain,
my family eluded rebel armies to flee

far north by foot on Ample-Flag Road.
By then, everyone we met had lost all

shame. Bird cries everywhere haunted
valleys, and no one was heading south.

My silly girl, starved, bit me hard and
screamed. Afraid of tigers and wolves,

I cradled her close and held her mouth:
she squirmed loose, wailed louder still.

Looking after us gallantly, my little boy
searched out sour-plum feasts for those

ten frantic days—half all thunderstorms
and mud we dragged ourselves through.

We didn't plan for rain. Sodden clothes
colder and colder, roads and paths slick,

we were often separated, and a full day
traveling took us but a few short miles.

Provisions gone, we lived on wild fruit,
low-hanging branches our only shelter,

left dew-splashed rocks before sunrise,
slept at the mist-laced edge of heaven.

We'd paused at Together-House Marsh,
planning to attempt Grass-Weave Pass,

when you took us in, old friend, your
kindness towering like billowed cloud.

Dusk gone dark, you hung lanterns out
and swung door after door wide open,

soothed our feet with hot tonic-baths,
cut paper talismans to lure our distant

spirits, then called wife and children,
their eyes pooling tender tears over us.

My chicks were soon asleep, but you
woke them with choice dishes of food,

offering toasts pledging the two of us
bound forever together like brothers,

and later you emptied out our rooms,
returning us to joy and peace and rest.

In these times overrun with calamity,
how many are so open and generous?

Now, a year of months later, Mongols
still spawning their grand catastrophes,

when will I lift off, feathers and wings,
and settle with you at the end of flight?

Jade-Blossom Palace

Beneath long pine winds, streams twist,
gray rats scuttle among ancient rooftiles:

I don't know whose palace this once was,
bequeathed beneath isolate cliffs to ruin,

its dark rooms flooded with blue ghost-
flame, its manicured paths washed away.

Earth's ten thousand sounds are the true
music. Autumn colors couldn't care less

about exquisite women, their rouge and
mascara sham that graced gold carriages

nothing but brown earth now. Of those
regal affairs, only a stone horse remains.

Sitting grief-stricken in wildgrass, I sing
wildly, wiping away tears: here amid this

sprawling journey of history's unfurling,
what would a rich and long life even be?

The Journey North

. . .

Heaven and Earth are racked with ruin,
sorrow and sorrow, and no end in sight.

I follow the road slowly into distances,
kitchen smoke rare, cold wind hissing,

and those I meet are mostly moaning
wounded, moaning and still bleeding.

I turn to watch dusk banners and flags
over Phoenix-Soar flare and smother,

then climb into cold mountain ridges,
stop to drink where war-horses water,

plunge to Riven-Altar's lowland fields
halved by cascading Deep-Flow River,

and suddenly I'm facing a fierce tiger,
its roar splitting ash-green cliffs apart.

Autumn-bright chrysanthemum petals
litter stone ancient war-carts scarred,

clouds billow into azure depths of sky:
O how quiet mystery contrives delight,

even now. Delicate jewels scattering
among acorn and chestnut, mountain

berries ripened to rich cinnabar reds,
blacks deep as lacquered bits of night:

what rain and dew bathe is everywhere
perfected fruit, whether bitter or sweet,

and Peach-Blossom longing is so easy,
that remorse over life's simplicity lost.

From high slopes I gaze at Deer-Altar,
cliffs breaking from vanishing valleys,

then hurry, making the river before my
servant's even left mountaintop forests.

Owls call from yellow mulberry trees,
marmots guard burrows, hands folded,

and soon in gaping night I cross battle-
fields, cold moon igniting white bones:

Pure-Water Pass warriors, how quickly
millions scattered there into the past,

and half our people followed them off,
the rest left mauled into strange things.

And I, too, caught in this Mongol dust,
I return with a crazed head of gray hair,

back home after a year to my thatch hut,
finding the family in patches and rags,

pine winds twisting sullen lament back,
brook murmuring grief in quiet mystery.

I've spent a lifetime pampering my boy,
and now he wears a face pale as snow:

seeing his dad without even socks, feet
dirt-and-grime, he turns away and cries.

Our two little girls keep near my bed,
robes pieced and sewn to cover knees,

patchwork oceans of billows and torn
waves, skewed odds and embroidered

ends beneath cloaks a purple-phoenix
potpourri among topsy-turvy sea gods.

An old heartsick man driven into bed,
vomiting and shitting for days—still,

I did manage a sack of silks for you,
no more shivering with cold, at least,

powder and mascara too, fancy wrap
already untied, and quilts all laid out.

My wife's bright-eyed again. Madcap
girls merrily comb at their hair. Elfin

studies of their mom, they smear dawn
makeup around in wild abandon: soon

rouge is flying everywhere, and they're
painting crazy demon-thick eyebrows.

Father returned large as life, these kids
almost forget hunger asking questions,

bickering and tugging my poor beard.
How could I scold them? Buffeted by

all the grief those warring rebels spawn,
I savor this racket, this wild clamoring.

Everyday want looming, and I scarcely
back to comfort them, what could I say?

.   .   .

Meandering River

Spring diminished with each petal in flight, I watch
wind scatter ten thousand flakes, grieving for all us

people. I want to exhaust blossoms vanishing here
into the eye, but can't bear wounds so profuse, so I

sip wine. Kingfishers nest in ruins along the river.
Dragon-horses doze among the park's regal tombs.

Search into the inner-pattern of things: isn't it joy?
Where is all this consequence tangling my life here?

2

Day after day, I pawn spring clothes when court ends
and return from the river thoroughly drunk. By now,

wine debts await me everywhere I go. But who ever
lives out life's seventy years? And today, butterflies

plunging deep into blooms shimmer deep in the eye.
Dragonflies in flight lazily ignite points along water,

and teaching insight whole, wind and light drift wide
where we here together in adoration will never part.

Dreaming of Li Po

Death at least gives separation repose.
Without death, its grief only sharpens.

You drift malarial southlands beyond
Yangtze distances, and I hear nothing,

exiled friend. Knowing I think of you
always now, you visit my dreams, my

heart frightened it isn't a living spirit
I dream. Fathomless miles: you come

so far from bright azure-green maples
night shrouds passes when you return,

and tangled as you are in nets of law,
with what bird's wings could you fly?

Flooding this room to the roof-beams,
the moon sinks. You linger in its light,

but the waters deepen into long swells,
dark dragons: take good care old friend.

Starveling Horse Chant

It wounds me: out among farmland fertility altars, a starveling
horse, bones poking out like a skeletal wall teetering near ruin,

tied tight. But it wants to range free, tugs and pulls at the rope,
and surely not to prance toward battle again in war-horse finery.

Looking closely, I see it's branded with government markings,
and people say the imperial armies left it here beside the road,

hide dry and peeling away, a desolate tangle of mud and mire,
fur stained with isolate silences of windblown snow and frost.

Last year they chased lingering rebels away in headlong waves,
and even grand stallions were useless if not seasoned in battle.

Our soldiers often ride prized horses taken from palace stables,
but surely you're one of those celestial steeds of ancient times

taken sick. Back then, out full-tilt across Mighty Mudball earth,
you must have stumbled and fallen, so this desertion was fated.

You gaze at me forlorn, as if crying out lament for a master lost,
for everything gone wrong and dark. No life lighting your eyes,

you're abandoned to far fields in winter, wild geese companions,
never brought in at night, crows pecking into wounds and sores.

In such ravaged times, who can tend you, wrap you in kindness,
who believe that next year spring grass will grow thick and tall?

For the Recluse, Eighth-Sentinel

Lives we humans live drift on without
ever meeting, like Scorpius and Orion,

so what could this night be, us together
here among candles and lamps radiant?

Youth never lasts long. And now, our
hair white, we ask after those we knew

back then, finding them mostly ghosts.
It startles the heart and smolders there.

Who dreamed it would be twenty years
before I came through your door again?

When we parted, you weren't married,
and suddenly there's a line of kids here,

gleefully honoring their father's friend,
asking where I came from. And before

madcap asking and telling end, they all
scamper away to serve wine and soup,

spring chives cut fresh in evening rain,
steam fresh-rice gracing yellow-millet.

Pronouncing reunions like this extinct,
you pour toasts ten cups each. Ten cups,

but it's your steady friendship keeps me
drunk. Tomorrow morning, between us

in this clamor of consequence, mountain
peaks will open out across two distances.

The Conscription Officer
at Stone-Channel

It was late, but he was out in the village
night rounding up men when I arrived.

Her worn-out old husband slipped away
over the wall, and she went to the gate.

The officer cursed loud and long, lost in
his rage. And lost in grief, an old woman

palsied with grief and tears, she pleaded:
My three sons went off to Flourish-Altar,

then finally, from one, a letter arrived
full of news: two killed in battle. Living

a stolen life, my last son can't last long,
and if you're dead you're forever dead

and gone. We've no men left—only my
baby grandson still at his mom's breast.

Coming and going, hardly half a ragged
skirt to put on, she can't leave him yet.

I'm old and weak, but I could hurry to
River-Brights with you tonight. Listen,

if you'd let me, I could be there in time,
cook an early meal for our brave boys.

Later, deep in long night, voices fade.
I almost hear crying hush into silence,

and morning, taking the road out front,
I find no one but the old man to leave.

Old-Age Farewell

Repose vanished in all four directions,
no one finds peace in old age anymore,

and I'm alone, my sons and grandsons
war-dead now, so why live out this life?

Tossing cane aside at my gate, I set out,
a grievous sight even to fellow soldiers:

lucky to have a few teeth left, but dust-
dry clear through to bone and marrow.

Lined up with young warriors in armor,
I offer long bows to some lofty official,

my old wife fallen by the road sobbing,
nothing but thin clothes against winter.

This is death's farewell, I know, and it
wounds me again with her bitter cold,

her plea that I *eat more, please*, though
no one ever returns from this departure.

Earth-Gate Wall is strong, and the river-
crossing at Apricot-Garden impossible,

but it's not the disaster at Flourish-Altar:
death is certain, but it's a long ways off.

Things come apart and come together:
why treasure one over the other in life,

but remembering us young and together,
I look back at her in this endless lament.

Nothing in ten thousand lands but war:
beacon-fires smother ridges and peaks,

the stench of death fills forest and field,
blood turns rivers and streams cinnabar

red, no village anywhere free of agony.
How can I hesitate, how avoid this life

torn from my quiet brambleweed home,
life now tattered in heart-stricken ruins?

WEST: REFUGEE LIFE BEGINS

(759)

S OON AFTER TU FU'S transfer, rebel armies began a new campaign that threatened the region where he was living. Tired of the bureaucratic struggle and leery of looming war, Tu resigned his position and moved his family into the far west: both to be far from the danger of renewed war, and as a commitment to poetry and a contemplative life. So begins the last eleven years of Tu Fu's existence: a period during which he lived as a wandering refugee moving further and further away from the center of his world and into the south, pushed ever onward by war, poverty, and a longing to return home to the north.

The conflict between a deeply felt responsibility to serve the government and a desire to live the more spiritually rewarding life of Taoist/Ch'an contemplation was a defining characteristic of China's artist-intellectuals, and many chose retirement sooner or later. But Tu Fu was remarkable in that he had no apparent means of support. This created considerable hardship for him and his family (though what would have happened had he stayed may have been far worse), but it also produced spectacular artistic results: not only were eighty percent of his poems written during this time, but their depth and complexity increased dramatically.

Thresh-Grain City was on the ethnic border between Chinese and tribal people, and Tibetans were also encroaching from the west. Fearful of the Tibetan armies and finding no relief from poverty complicated by a relapse of his malaria, Tu moved to Gather Valley (p. 81) in search of a more secure life. But after six weeks of continuing poverty, the family again set out—this time on a five-hundred-mile winter journey to Al-tar-Whole City (today's Chengdu) in far southwest China. The family had little food, and the journey was grueling: in addition to fording a

number of dangerous rivers, they had to make a perilous mountain cross-
ing that included a road so precarious that numerous stretches were actually
wooden structures suspended on the sides of large cliffs (p. 89).

Getting Free of Thoughts

I dismount on the old battlefield, gaze
through four directions of blank waste:

wind-moans and clouds drifting away,
yellow leaves scattering down across

rotting bones gnawed through by ants
and smothered by vines in late bloom.

Sage-elders lamented all this long ago,
but clerks can't stop opening frontiers,

so those enemies and us win and lose
by turns. And borders shift, then shift

again. Where's a general so masterful
our soldiers can sleep their days away?

Thresh-Grain Songs

2

North of Thresh-Grain City, a monastery
amid Clamor-Exalt's rebel-palace ruins:

halls painted cinnabar and azure empty,
ancient mountain-gate lichen and moss.

Moonlit dew flares on leaves tumbling.
Clouds chase wind across wild streams.

Lone clarity heartless in desperate times,
Moon-Field River just flows away east.

4

As night falls at the river's source, war
drums and horns emerge from border-

land origins, rising from autumn earth,
scattered on wind into clouds, grieving.

Cold cicadas fallen silent clutch leaves.
A bird returns lazily to mountain home.

It's like this in all ten thousand districts:
how could my road ever end in arrival?

10

Ch'i-cloud stretches to Bright-Posterity
Mountain, and frontier rain sheets down.

Tribal boys gaze into Moon-Field River.
Regal envoys near Yellow River origins.

Cook-smoke trails out over army camps,
oxen and sheep amid ridgeline villages:

just now, autumn grass grown suddenly
still here, I close my little bramble gate.

12

On the summit, South-Rim Monastery
at a creek called North-Flow: ancient

tree appearing in the empty courtyard,
flume carrying clear water to a village.

Autumn blossoms beneath risky cliffs,
late shadow near a fallen bell: looking,

looking grieves for this self and world,
stream-sliced wind gusting our lament.

17

Frontier autumn: nights become such *yin-*
dark morning radiance may never return.

Rain confusions off eaves tangle curtains,
mountain cloud tumbling across our wall,

and cormorants peer into a shallow well.
Worms climb deep indoors. It's desolate

horse-cart silence. But out past our gate,
the hundred grasses stretch far and away.

Moonlit Night, Thinking of My Brothers

Warning drums have ended all travel.
A lone goose cries across borderland

autumn. Dew first chills frost-white
tonight. This moon's bright over our

old village, my brothers scattered, no
home to ask if they're alive or dead.

Letters sent never arrive. War comes
and goes—then comes like this again.

At Sky's End, Thinking of Li Po

Cold wind breaks out here at sky's end:
so what is it you're thinking, old friend?

How could geese ever bring news, now
autumn floods drown rivers and lakes?

Art resents life fulfilled, forest demons
feed on travelers with delight: why not

sink poems deep into Sun-Weave River,
talk things over with that ill-used ghost?

Overnight at Master Illumine's House

How did your abbot-staff ever get you here?
Autumn winds already a desolate moan, rain

tangles depths of courtyard chrysanthemums,
and in the pond, frost topples lotus blossoms.

Cast into exile, you never abandon original-
nature. Emptiness empty, you keep close to

ch'an stillness. All night long, we share this
ridge-dragon moon facing us round and full.

Rain Clears

Here at sky's edge, autumn cloud thins
away on ten-thousand-mile west winds.

It's a lovely morning: sky clear, land lit,
farmers no longer mired in endless rain.

Frontier willows air kingfisher-greens.
Red fruit flecks mountain-pear. Mongol

flute-song off the tower, then one goose
climbs clear through empty-sky depths.

View in the Eye

The whole land through: ripened grapes
and mountain pastures lavish in autumn,

clouds and steady rain shrouding passes,
frontier streams swollen almost to rivers.

Tribal women tease away at beacon-fires.
Mongol boys lead camels about. Enough,

eyes wounded by eventual dark, all loss
and ruin: of what comes to pass, enough.

Getting Free of Thoughts

My grief-stricken eyes find frost, wild-
bloom chrysanthemums on city-walls,

whole-sky winds battering at willows.
There's clear flute-song, traveler tears,

tower-shadow straight into still water,
frontier light aslant in mountain dusk.

Birds return into darkness, then come
slaughter-filled cries: crows settling-in.

First Moon

Thin slice of ascending light, radiant arc
tipped aside bellied dark—the first moon

appears and, barely risen beyond ancient
frontier passes, edges into clouds. Silver,

changeless, the Star River spreads across
mountains empty in their own cold. Lucent

frost dusts the courtyard, chrysanthemum
blossoms clotted there with swollen dark.

Pounding Clothes

Frontiers return no one, I know, but
it's autumn, season of fulling-stones.

Already, a bitter cold moon sharpens
separation's long ache. I exhaust my

woman's strength here at home, send
clothes deep into Great Wall country.

I pound and pound, and you my love
listen to sounds beyond empty skies.

Standing Alone

Empty skies. And beyond, one hawk.
Between riverbanks, two white gulls

laze wind-drifted. Fit for an easy kill,
to and fro, they follow contentment.

Grasses all frost-singed. Spiderwebs
still hung. Heaven's loom of origins

tangling our human ways too, I stand
facing sorrow's ten thousand sources.

Gazing into Wildlands

Autumn clarity opens boundless away:
yin-dark rises far off, layers thickening,

distant river empties into flawless sky,
lone city-walls vanish in depths of fog.

The last few leaves scattering on wind,
sun sinking away among remote peaks:

why so late, this lone crane returning?
Crows already glut forests with night.

Empty Purse

Bitter kingfisher-green juniper berries
and high dawn-lit cirrus: they're fine

food for immortals. But we people are
common things, this tangle of trouble

my only life: no stove, well-water ice
mornings, frosty nights without quilts.

Afraid my empty purse is ashamed of
poverty, I keep one coin on view inside.

Salt Wells

Grasses and trees are white in this salt
realm, salt-smoke blackest green-azure,

salt-boiling smoke shrouding the river
to meet government demands. Workers

haul up salty water all year, feed fires,
and all day send out loaded wagons: it

earns officials three hundred a jar, then
six hundred for merchants. You noble-

minded ones will never stop at enough,
and people's grief just clamors on. So,

why such lament? It's the inner-pattern,
isn't it, occurrence appearing of itself?

Dharma-Mirror Monastery

Lives imperiled, we left for this new land.
Steady struggle's only brought bitter grief,

and traveling mountain depths wounds me.
But sorrows end in a cliffwall monastery's

old ways: graceful emerald-lichen purities,
chilled bamboo-sheaths crackling in wind,

wild churn of mountain-root streamwater,
thin rain misting slow across pine treetops

as faint-haze cloud hides morning clarities.
The sun rises veiled—then breaking clear

ignites half the red-tile roof incandescent,
reveals precise doors and window-lattices.

I lean on a staff, forgetting what's to come,
and it's noon before I step inside the gate.

A cuckoo deep in far-sky shadow calls out:
this, isn't this where my sparse path ends?

Azure-Brights Gorge

I'm sick of mountains beyond borderlands,
and it's worse on these roads leading south.

Ridge and summit tangling away together,
cloud and stream a single confusion of *ch'i*,

I come through distant forests into a chisel-
edge gorge, skies narrow, cliffwalls hacked

flat: five miles of rock up west of the creek
looming in a rage and tumbling toward me,

I watch the sun-carriage tilted askew above
and Earth's pivot down below gone feeble.

People-eating forest demons howl in wind,
frost-and-sleet expanses open out vast away:

I dreaded crossing Dragon-Back Mountain,
facing high Clamor Peak autumn. But come

here, I laugh. Lotus-Flourish Peak far away
east tiny, Empty-Tribe meager in the north:

transcendent and equal to the fiercest gaze,
they flourish boundless with isolate silence,

lofty and adamantine, and yet following me
even now—wondrous in their dark stillness.

Seven Songs at Gather Valley

I

A wanderer—O all year a wanderer named Tu Fu,
white hair a shoulder-length confusion, gathering

acorns all year, like that monkey sage. Under cold
sky, the sun sets in this mountain valley. No word

arrives from the central plains, and for my failing
skin and bone, my ice-parched hands and feet, no

return, no return there Song, my first song
                              sung, O song already sad enough,
winds come from the furthest sky grieving my grief.

2

Sturdy hoe—O long sturdy hoe, my white-timbered
fortune: now we're depending on you, on you alone

for life, there's hardly a wild yam-shoot to dig. Snow
fills the mountains. I tug at this coat never covering

my shins. And when I come home empty-handed
again, my children's cries are deafening, four walls

harboring quiet Song, my second song
                              sung, O song beginning to carry,
this village is peopled with the faces of my sorrow.

3

Brothers of mine, my brothers in far-off places—O
three thin brothers grown frail and weak, and these

scattered lives we wander never meet, Mongol dust
smothering sky, roads between us going on forever.

Cranes flock eastward, following geese. But cranes,
how could cranes carry me there, to that life beside

my brothers Song, my third song
                                sung, O song sung three times over,
who knows where they'll come to gather my bones?

4

Sister of mine, sister away in Gather-Apart, husband
dead young, orphan children unhinged—O my sister:

the long Gale River all deep-swell flood-dragon fury,
how could you come now? And after ten years, how

will I find you in my little boat? Arrows fill my eyes,
and southlands riddled with war's banners and flags

harbor another dark Song, my fourth song
                              sung, O song rehearsed four times through,
gibbons haunt midday forest light wailing my wails.

5

Four mountains all windswept, headlong streams and
rain—O the cold rain falling through bare trees falls,

and clouds hang low. Among brown weeds, deserted
city-walls: white foxes prowl, brown foxes keep still.

This life of mine, how can I live out this life in some
starveling valley? I sit up all night long, ten thousand

worries gathering Song, my fifth song
                                    sung, O song already long enough
calling my spirit, my lost spirit gone to my lost home.

6

Dragon—O dragon in southern mountains, cragged
trees tangling their ancient branches above its pool:

when yellowed leaves fall, it sinks into hibernation,
and from the east come vipers prowling the waters.

A traveler amazed they would dare show themselves,
I slice them apart with my sword, and once I finish I

rest here Song, my sixth song
                           sung, O song wearing thoughts thin,
streams and valleys are me again graced with spring,

7

                              me a man
every distinction has eluded, a man grown old only
to wander three hungry years along mountain roads.

Palace ministers are young now. Honor and wealth:
we devote ourselves early. Wise men I knew there:

they live in these mountains now. Our talk's all old
times gone by, nothing more: old friends harboring

wounded memories Song, my seventh song
                              sung, O uneasy silence ending my tune,
white sun empties majestic sky with headlong flight.

River-Swarm Crossing

This mountain journey has set stages,
but it's past midnight, a sparse moon

sunk hours ago, and still we can't rest.
After a road tipped askew down cliffs,

a vast river suddenly surged before us,
billows boundless as ocean expanses.

Inner-pattern in motion, the boatman
sang out, laughing at seething waves,

at frost glistening across rock and tree,
wind headlong, hands and feet frozen.

Our thousand fears at that ferry: they
twist ten thousand times on this high

summit. But gazing out beyond flood-
waters, I realize how parched stars are.

And me? Left a wraith by this distant
travel, thin and sick: should I eat less?

Immortal-Flight Trestle-Road

On Earth-Gate Mountain things get tight:
the sparse road up thins to an autumn hair,

then turns into precarious trestle-and-rail
bolted along cliffwalls high among cloud.

Ten thousand gorges through empty trees,
cascades tumbling deep layers of *yin*-dark:

far from a winter sun's serenity, we keep
struggling on where boundless winds rage.

Only when we pause in a valley, only then
do we realize what heights we've crossed,

and how it's exhausted family and horses,
all this leaving, no chance for rest or sleep.

Drifting dream-life all gather and scatter,
hunger and plenty: no one eludes it. Still,

in sad wonder, I say to my wife and kids:
how did you talk me into this lunatic trek?

SOUTHWEST: VILLAGE LIFE

(760–765)

THE TU FAMILY finally reached Altar-Whole early in 760. Altar-Whole was the largest city in western China, and Tu Fu found a number of well-placed friends and relatives there, including the provincial governor. With their generous assistance, he built a comfortable house in a small village outside the city. It was a quiet farming village, but there were a number of like-minded artist-intellectuals there, and a Ch'an monastery where the Tu family stayed while their house was built. The poet spent two happy years in this village. Though there were times of hardship when patrons moved away or died, and his poor health continued (severe rheumatism complicating his chronic struggle with asthma and recurring malaria), Tu had finally found the quiet contemplative life of a country recluse that he had long desired.

After two years, a local rebellion broke out. Tu fled east to another city in the region, Village-Tree, where he stayed several years before he could move back to his village. Tu remained in the village for another year, though it wasn't quite so tranquil a time as the first two years. The rebellion in the north was finally defeated in early 763, ending the cataclysmic civil war, but not the chronic militarism it generated. In addition to local rebellions throughout the country, Tibetans became a constant threat from the west. Indeed, they controlled territory in the Altar-Whole region, and Tu became a military advisor, often staying in the city to help the provincial governor defend the region. Finally, with the death of the governor and another local rebellion looming, Tu Fu set out with his family down the Yangtze River into the southlands of China.

Ch'i-Siting Our New House

Here beside Bathe-Flower Stream, the stream's west bank,
our diviner finds the site near a forest pond's quiet mystery.

I knew leaving the city would end the dust of human affairs,
but there's all this clear water too, and it eases refugee grief:

countless dragonflies dipping and soaring in a single skein,
a lazy pair of harlequin ducks drifting and diving together.

From here I can journey ten thousand miles east *on a whim*:
just sail a little boat off to *yin*-dark Mountain-Shadow home.

Asking a Friend to Find Me Some Pine Starts

Standing alone, austere, not at all willow,
azure-green nothing like plum: I imagine

old age nurtured in thousand-year shade.
Please find sturdy ones, with frosty roots.

Our House Is Done

Its back to the city and thatched in white, our house is done.
River road bowing through green fields: you know the way,

and here there's goat-willow shade, leaves whispering wind,
dragon-bamboo gathering river-mist into leaf-tip dewdrops.

Crows in wandering flight pause, tend their clutch of chicks.
Arriving in a rush, talkative swallows settle into new nests.

Passersby might think it the home of some ancient poet-sage,
but life's idle here, mind empty: who needs to write poems?

Cut-Short Poems

1

Sun rising from water east of our fence,
mud breathes out mist north of the house.

High in bamboo: kingfisher cry. Below,
on shoreline sand: magpie mating-dance.

2

Pollen blossoms a lavish confusion every-
where, bees and butterflies in busy flight:

I perch in quiet mystery here, all idleness.
What was it like—that longing for arrival?

3

Palm leaves cover the new well, where
ditches run through bamboo root away.

Rigging sways delicately on riverboats,
and footpaths weave into village depths.

4

Stream swollen after headlong rain, late
slant-light wraps a tree's waist. Yellow

birds, one pair, keep hidden in their nest.
Where reeds shudder, a white fish leaps.

5

Below the house, bamboo needles walls.
In the courtyard, wisteria crowds eaves.

Fields turning slowly to sunlit silk, reeds
weave the white river in tracery shadow.

6

River sweeps moonlight across stone.
Stream empties mist-fringed blossoms.

Perched birds understand ancient Way.
Sails pass, spend night in whose home?

A Guest Stops By

I've battled seized lung-*ch'i* for years,
but this *ch'i*-sited river house is new:

simple sounds far from noise, healing
joy and ease infusing our thatch eaves.

Whenever a guest stops by, I call our
kids to get my farm hat on right, then

thin vegetables with a hoe, gather fine
thinnings: a few handfuls of friendship.

Cut-Short Poems

Bamboo tall west of the house, I stop opening the gate.
Peppers in rows north of the waterway, I give up town.

When they ripen, Red-Wood and I will feast on plums.
When pines tower, I'll discuss it with Origins-Abound.

I long to build a fishing pier, but clouds tumble and churn
wild water here, and this fourth-moon rain too sounds cold.

Dragons settled this black-azure stream first: even sturdy as
mountains, how could bamboo and stone ever comfort me?

3

Two yellow orioles fill kingfisher-green willows with song.
Egrets climb away into crystalline skies, lone trail of white.

At my window: thousand-autumn snows on western peaks.
At my gate: boats bound ten thousand miles to eastern seas.

River Village

In a lone curve, cradling our village, the clear river
flows past. All summer long, the business of quiet

mystery fills this river village. Nesting in the eaves,
carefree swallows come and go. On the water, gulls

nestle together. My wife draws a paper chessboard,
and tapping at needles, the kids contrive fishhooks.

Often sick, I need drugs and herbs—but what more,
come to all this, what more could a sparse man ask?

Our Farmhouse

Clear river curves past our farmhouse:
brushwood gate beside an ancient road,

wildgrass grown over market and well.
I'm idle, dress however I please in this

simple place. Aimless willow branches
sway. Loquat scents air—tree after tree.

Drying spread wings in western sun, lit
fisher-cormorants crowd along our pier.

River Flooding

River flooding at my brushwood gate,
kids come shouting about wild water:

it's feet higher before I'm out of bed,
then with a cane, I watch islands sink.

Swallows greet wind in delicate arcs.
Seagulls buffeted lightly chase waves.

Swirling his tiny paddle, a fisherman
turns the boat's prow effortlessly true.

Wildland Old-Timer

Wildland old-timer, riverbank bending along my bamboo fence,
I open tumbledown brushwood gates, and set out along the river:

fishermen gather out their nets from a pool of crystalline depths,
a trader's boat trailing after dusk's failing flare comes drifting in.

Our long journey: Sword-Tower Peak now frontier-mind lament.
What could explain it: me a flake of cloud at this *Ch'in* Terrace?

Imperial armies haven't pronounced those eastern provinces safe,
and atop city-wall gates, autumn beginning, painted horns grieve.

Towering Kindred-Tree

The color of far-sky depths, a kindred-tree
at the river spreads its green-azure canopy.

I planted our herb garden beside its roots,
built a thatch pavilion touching its leaves.

Its shadow whole even in slant dusk light,
its harmonies singing out in sparse winds:

whenever I find myself dead drunk, I doze
beneath it, and suddenly I'm utterly sober.

Playful Song About a Landscape Painting

Ten days to paint a single river;
                                 five days to paint a single rock:
a skill that won't be hurried by anything, that's how it begins,

how such masters transmit clarity absolute. What magisterial
strength, this sprawl from Queen Goddess's western summits

to that sea-isle of immortals, all spread beneath high ceilings
here on your wall colored pale with origins. Open-Hand Ridge,

Goddess-Court Lake, sun-source Japan seas: Yangtze flowing
through and up into the Star River, *ch'i*-cloud trails out behind

dragons in flight, boatmen and fishermen drift near shorelines,
mountain forests heave beneath winds churning up vast waves.

Nothing ancient compares to such mastery of limitless terrain:
a mere foot spans ten thousand miles! If I could somehow find

scissors of razor-sharp Gather-Land steel, I would shear away
half those Clamor-Pine River distances, claim them for keeps!

Morning Rain

Hissing in dawn light, cold *ch'i*-gale
tattering river-cloud buffets eyesight.

Wind-ducks shelter in island havens,
rain-swallows wait in thicket refuge:

Gauze, Yellow, Nest, Source: ancient
sages refused emperors good and bad.

Thatch hut, last wine—lingering out
this clear morning gathers me in joy.

Madman

At my thatch hut west of Ten-Thousand-Mile Bridge,
you can drift all change on Hundred-Flower Stream.

Kingfisher-green bamboo sways—elegant, flawless.
Red lotus blossoms in rain grow even more fragrant.

Old friends with fat salaries gave up sending letters,
and kids, forever hungry, wear faces of cold despair.

About to fill some ditch, he is carefree, the madman
grown old laughing at his growing steadily madder.

Our Southern Neighbor

A master of this brocade land, he sports a crow-peaked hat,
and he's still not destitute: there's garden taro and chestnut,

and well-versed hosts, his children entertain with abandon.
Even young birds, dining on front steps, feel at home there.

The river's swollen now, four or five feet of autumn water,
and boats here hold two or three people. Dusk falls in this

river village: white sand, kingfisher-green bamboo. When
we part, moonlight touches my brushwood gate all anew!

Hundred Worries Gathering Chant

My heart's young again, remembering my fifteenth year:
I was strong as a brown calf scampering here and there

in the courtyard. It was the eighth moon, pears and dates
ripe, and I scrambled up a thousand times in a single day.

How suddenly it all passed. I'm already fifty, and barely
ever walk or even get up. If not asleep, I sit still, resting.

Visiting friends, forcing laughter and small-talk, I grieve
over a hundred worries gathering here at the edge of life,

and when I return home, everything's the same as ever:
cupboards empty, old wife sharing the look on my face.

Silly kids, still ignorant of the ritual esteem due a father:
angry, screaming at the kitchen door, they demand food.

Brimmed Whole

I

Boundless wilds of country sun radiant,
spring floods such confusions of clarity.

Rushes along islands: that they are there!
And paths among village gates, perfect!

True to carefree ways, clothes deranged,
I follow that sage of cap-strained wine.

Clear to the end of sight: flawless. Even
sick many times over, my body is light.

2

It's already mid-spring on the riverbank,
blossoms fallen, and sun still rises clear.

Hearing a bird, I look up to find nothing.
Turning back, I answer . . . no one there.

I read, skipping over hard parts with ease,
pour wine from always full jars. That old

Eyebrow Mountain sage is a new friend:
he knows it is here, in idleness, I am real.

Plum Rains

Fourth-moon plums, ripe and yellow, line
Buffalo-Creek Road to our city of brocade.

Deep and clear, this long river flows away.
Out of dark distant skies, light rains arrive,

soaking easily through loose roofing thatch,
and these lowering clouds won't clear soon.

All day long, dragons delight: swells coil
and surge into banks, then startle back out.

Out in the Boat

Farming southern fields near our city of brocade, a refugee
still, I sit at the north window, spirit-wounded, gazing north.

Today, my wife and I climb into a little river-boat. Drifting,
skies clear, we watch our kids play in such crystalline water,

butterflies chasing each other tumbling together through air,
and sharing stalks, lotus flowers in intimate pairs blooming.

Tea, sugar-cane juice: we brought along what simple things
we have, nothing fancy, our clay jars no less now than jade.

Autumn Wind Ravaging Thatch House Song

It's the eighth moon, high autumn, and suddenly a raging wind
breaks loose, howling, whirling three layers of rooftop thatch
away: thatch soaring across the river, scattering into fieldlands,

some bundles buffeted so high they litter lofty forest treetops
and some whirled so low they sink sodden into pond bottoms.

Then a band of kids shows up from the south village,
                                   and seeing how old and feeble I am,
they know they can face me as robbers and thieves in the open,
so they gather up our thatch and soon vanish into the bamboo.

I yell until lips and throat feel parched as fire—but it's no good,
so I come back home, propped on a cane and sighing to myself,

then the wind goes suddenly still, and clouds swell dark as ink,
autumn skies vast and silent deepening to black, as dusk arrives.

We've used our quilts so many years. They're cold as iron now,
and our sweet kids tear them open, sleeping fitfully and kicking,

kicking, leaks dribbling everywhere, all the beds, nowhere dry,
rain sheeting down like flax: sheeting down, and no end in sight.

I've lived years of loss and ruin, and rarely slept well, but what
would make sense of this unending rain-drenched night? How

could there ever be a vast palace, a thousand-ten-thousand-room
grand shelter for cold people everywhere throughout
                                   all beneath heaven, joyful faces smiling,
shelter unyielding through wind and rain, steady as a mountain?

O when
will I see that palace home regal and majestic right here
before my very eyes? Then, yes,
then I'd be content freezing to death in this ravaged
thatch hut, alone and more than content.

Lament for My Kindred-Tree Torn Down by Raging Wind and Rain

Standing beside the river in front of my thatch hut, this
kindred-tree old-timers swear is two hundred years old:

it's the whole reason I *ch'i*-sited a house and cut thatch
here, its wintry cicada-song in midsummer's heat-haze.

But a swirling southwest wind came, shaking the earth,
seething *ch'i*-cloud churning river and scattering stone,

thunder and rain. The trunk pushed back, strength fierce,
but roots were torn away from deep springs. How is this

ch'i-mind unfurling? I loved azure-deep waves and tree,
this lone green-azure canopy draped out over the stream,

lingered beneath it, wildland guest amid frost and snow,
and passersby rare, I listened to its pipes and flutes sing.

Tiger head-over-heels, dragon toppled-out upside-down:
it's cast among thorn brambles, my tears on robes blood-

stained. Where will I ever go to chant new poems now?
And beauty that enchants: it's finished at this thatch hut.

Alone, Looking for Blossoms Along the River

1

Who understands the grief these riverside blossoms inflict?
It makes me crazy, and there's no one here to tell, so I go

searching for our southern neighbor, my old friend in wine,
but he's gone ten days drinking. All I find is an empty bed.

2

A thick frenzy of blossoms crowding our river shorelines,
I wander along, listing dangerously, in full fear of spring.

With poems and wine against all that profusion, I endure:
arrangements for this ancient, white-haired man can wait.

3

Deep river repose, two or three houses in bamboo quiet,
and such goings-on: red blossoms blazing among white.

Answering spring's radiant glories, I too have my place:
sending them off with a lovely wine on the shores of life.

4

Looking east to the city all smoke crowded with blossoms,
I love our little Hundred-Flower Stream tower even more:

to open gold jars and ladle out fine wine, calling beautiful
women to dance on embroidered mats: who could bear it?

5

At the monastery abbot's grave, the river flows away east,
spring's radiant glories idle and tired among sparse winds.

In this crush of peach blossoms open without their owner's
empty mind, I can treasure reds deep or shallow the same.

6

Blossoms crowd orchard paths where the abbot's wife lives:
thousands, tens of clustered thousands weigh branches down,

and ceaseless butterflies linger in playful dance, as exquisite
oriole song tumbles along empty and altogether its very self.

7

This love of blossoms: it isn't longing for death. It's fear,
fear that once they're gone, old age will overwhelm me,

and they scatter away easily, by the branchful. Let's talk
things over, little buds: open meticulously, languorously.

Wandering at Cultivate-Aware Monastery

Wildland monastery, river and sky open,
mountain gate in bamboo-and-blossom

quiet mystery. Gods must aid my poems:
how else could I wander here in spring?

Paths and rocks snake around each other.
River and cloud of themselves go or stay.

Birds roost on branches of *ch'an* stillness,
but I leave at dusk buffeted in grief adrift.

A Guest Arrives

South of our house, and north: it's everywhere spring
water, nothing to see but gulls arriving day after day.

Courtyard path all blossoms not yet swept for guests:
today, for you, I open my bramble gate this first time.

Dinners this far out from market are nothing special,
and wine in our beggarly home is old and unstrained,

but if you'll drink with the old-timer living next door,
I'll call over the fence, invite him to share what's left.

A Farmer

In this land of brocade, no dust or smoke,
our river village has eight or nine homes,

waterlily leaves floating, tiny and round,
delicate wheat blossoms feathering away.

I'll grow old here in this *ch'i*-sited house,
a farmer far from that world of confusion,

and no interest at all in ancient alchemy,
its cinnabar drugs promising endless life.

Spring Night, Delighting in Rain

Knowing their season, lovely rains
appear in spring. They enter night

secretly on the winds, and silently
adorn things in gossamer shimmers.

Clouds ink country lanes with dark.
A lone riverboat lamp. Then dawn

opens glistening reds everywhere:
our blossom-laden city of brocade.

Thoughts Brimful: Cut-Short Poems

1

Eyes drunk on all this wanderer's grief, I can't wake from
grief, and shifty spring color still crowds into my river hut.

Blossoms opening confusion this deep and reckless might
at least teach orioles to tone down all their yammering joy.

2

I planted peach and plum myself: they're not ownerless.
Courtyard walls are low: but it's home to an old hermit.

So like spring wind, never letting things alone: last night
it came wailing, tearing blossoms down by the branchful.

3

Knowing full well how cozy my little thatch library is,
quick swallows over the river come gliding in nonstop:

beaks clutching mud, they spatter *ch'in* and books, and
darting at insects, crash into whoever dares appear here.

4

The second moon in ruins, a third arrives. You grow old
slowly, it's true, but how many springs could I have left?

Those inexhaustible workings beyond me: I leave them
alone—just empty this cup full of life's lingering limits.

5

It's heartbreaking—river spring beginning its end. I stroll
along, goosefoot cane and all, stop among fragrant shores.

Unhinged willow seed-fluff tumbles dancing after wind,
and thoughtless peach blossoms trail riverwater on away.

6

Indolent and idle, I never leave the village. When I call
my kids, they've long-since closed our brushwood gate.

Moss green, wine thick: here amid trees, quiet gathers.
Jade-pure water. Spring winds. Out beyond fields, dusk.

7

Scattered poplar blossoms carpet paths here with white.
Green coins in piles, waterlily leaves fleck streamwater.

Baby pheasants among bamboo roots: no one sees them.
Close beside mothers on riverbank sand, ducklings doze.

8

West of the house, you can pick delicate mulberry leaves,
and along river paths, wheat's elegant finery sways again.

How many times can spring turn summer in this one life?
Never give it up: waste wine fragrant and sweet as honey.

9

Delicate willows swaying outside my door—slender,
graceful as a girl's waist at fifteen: who was it saying

just another morning, same as ever? That wild wind
broke them down: the longest, most elegant branches.

At Manifold-Devotion Post-Station, a Second Farewell to the Governor

Ending our distant farewell, separation
begins here, green mountains emptiness

felt. We'll never again wander together
sipping wine beneath last night's moon.

The whole country sings praises of you,
radiant through three reigns. Me, I'll go

home to my river village, nurture what
life remains in isolate depths of silence.

9/9 Festival: On the City-Wall at Village-Tree

This night of long-life yellow-blossom
wine finds me old, my hair white. Joy,

the strength to chase joy seems foreign,
and years passing blur in distant views.

Brothers and sisters filling my desolate
chants, Heaven and Earth drunken eyes,

warriors and weapons, frontier passes:
all this thought today beyond knowing.

Propped on a Cane

I crave blossoms, so even here in the city
I wander streambanks propped on a cane.

Markets close up early in these mountains.
It's spring. Riverboats gather at the bridge,

fearless gulls frolicking amid whitewater
and homeward geese relishing blue skies.

All things share life's *ch'i*-mind impulse,
why not wintry brooding over lost years?

Gazing at Ox-Head Mountain Monastery

It's Buddha's White-Crane death-grove:
Steps wind into depths quiet in mystery

here, spring colors float beyond peaks,
Star River fills meditation-hall shadow.

Sun-bright Absence transmits the lamp;
yellow-gold Presence reveals the earth.

No more this song-wild old man, I turn
and gaze into mind that dwells nowhere.

Wall-Painting of Cranes at the Whole-Springs District Offices

A master's eleven cranes, all painted
absolute in green-azure-field clarity:

colors long-since faded into silvered
ash-dark, but far from dust, the birds

high and low, each with its *ch'i*-mind
precision, deep as sage-elder insight.

I marvel over the *ch'i*-distances their
attention opens: how could it be mere

pigment? Flying ten thousand miles
with ease, they roam kindred in thick

flocks—majestic as white phoenixes,
nothing at all like orioles and the rest.

Before this high hall fell broken into
ruins, they comforted refugee guests:

now they're left out to the elements,
lament for ravages of wind and rain,

while real cranes soar dusk-lit cloud
free of a surging and swelling world,

trusting themselves to far-sky depths
anywhere they like. What tames that?

Climbing with Four Governors to Meaning-Bestow Monastery

Spring day in borderlands beyond people,
sky all emptiness empty dwells nowhere.

Orioles and blossoms all time and space
alive, my tower room faces ranged peaks

as eventual dark falls. Who fathoms self?
Climbing to gaze out, bewildered and lost,

can you forget renown's gold name-seals,
sit smiling wild and share *ch'an* stillness?

Setting the Boat Free

I bid friends farewell at Silver-Ash Creek.
The mountains are cold, no let up in rain,

and I worry it's too slippery for my horse,
so I take the boat drifting back homeward:

green-azure endearing peaks and summits,
yellows promising ripe orange and citron.

River flowing boundless poise—I sit still,
mind carried vast into its distances away.

Thatch Hut

When I left this thatch hut so long ago,
mongrel armies filled our brocade city,

and today, as I return to this thatch hut,
it's peace that crowds our brocade city.

Can I tell you how disaster broke loose,
how it all turned suddenly upside down?

Our great general had left for the palace,
and that band of thugs schemed betrayal,

knifed a white horse one night, crazed,
and smeared their mouths in blood-oath,

then gathered Skill-Altar South armies,
cut off Sword-Tower road in the north,

and scores of common people followed,
crowding inside gates to occupy the city.

There can't be two powers in such times:
soon Tibetans and Chinese were arguing,

soldiers out west turned on one another,
and rebel officials executed each other:

how could they savage themselves like
owl and wildcat, children eating parents?

People of principle were heart-stricken
how law and order were broken beyond

chaos—our homeland with three lords,
the ten thousand people food for fish.

Chanting praises of imperial majesty,
convinced no one was guilt-free, they

lined people up in fetters and shackles,
pipes and flutes serenading out behind,

then laughing and chatting slaughtered
all, splashing blood flooding avenues:

where axes swung, you can still hear
wailing and moaning in wind and rain,

courtesans and horses become ghosts
too, old pleasure now faces of sorrow.

Our homeland's rule of law still intact,
all this amazed everyone into grieving

lament, and I fled, a master of poverty,
longed three years to sail far southeast,

but bows and arrows darkened over our
river-and-sea lands, the five lakes lost,

and I needed this village, so I've come
back to clear briars and weeds. I open

gates to find these four pines still here,
wander my ten thousand airy bamboo.

Our ancient dog delights in my return,
frisks around, sneaks in under my robe,

and the neighbors delight in my return,
bring wine to this tribal hovel of mine.

Lofty officials too delight in my return,
send riders to ask after our every need,

and the whole city delights in my return,
everyone crowding into the village here.

All beneath heaven nowhere near peace,
fierce warriors mean more than savants:

so, adrift at the edge of windblown dust,
where would an old-timer like me settle?

These days it's all infection and canker,
but I'm happy, bones not dried marrow,

even if I am derelict. No wine; and food:
why hope for any more than thorn-bean?

Cut-Short Poem

After a walk along the river's green-azure,
I turn away and gaze at banners and flags.

Winds rise. It's spring, dusk over the city,
horns and drums on high towers grieving.

Life Hidden Away

In simplicity, I nurture Way my own way.
In quiet mystery, things seen are thoughts

felt: mulberry and hemp all rain and dew,
swallows and sparrows midway into life,

village war-drums day-by-day throbbing,
fishing boats one-by-one light as air. My

hair all white, goosefoot cane: what joy,
mind and life gone perfectly transparent!

Leaving the City

It's bone-bitter cold, and late, and falling
frost traces my gaze all bottomless skies.

Smoke trails out over distant salt mines.
Snow-covered peaks slant shadows east.

Armies haunt my homeland still, and war
drums throb in this far-off place. A guest

overnight here in this river city, I return
again to shrieking crows, my old friends.

Spring Day, River Village

I came far distances into these four-river
lands. Six years have slipped away here:

I'm a visitor, but friends are old friends
now, forests and streams surging elation,

and all idleness, I relish patched clothes,
wander happy in these shoes worn bare.

This bamboo fence perfectly boundless,
ch'i-mind empty, I gaze into river skies.

On the Stream, Adrift

Tower casting shadow: my boat drifts
across its dark and far upstream. Who

says village life is pinched? It goes on
out here, west of stately village trees:

deserted fieldland opens into distances,
autumn color sharpening cold clarities,

mountaintop snow bleached sun-glare
silk. Gossamer rainbow lighting cloud,

children frolic on banks left and right,
wielding nets and fish-spears, churning

confusions of lotus and water-chestnut,
and giving directions that leave me lost.

They quickly scale any fish they catch,
but leave lotus-root covered with mud:

people crave things fresh and beautiful,
but not here among these simple things.

My village lovely under dusk-lit cloud,
neighbors' chickens settled-in by now:

where am I going in this isolate silence,
now leaving and staying scarcely differ?

I watch new moonlight ignite my robes
and climb field-wall ruins beneath frost:

pauper-wine ready as ever to soothe us,
war-drums break-out on city-walls east.

Overnight at the War-Office

War-office in clear autumn, cold kindred-tree at the well:
I'm here overnight in this river city, candles guttering low,

alone. In the forever dark, grieving horns call to each other,
and moon drifts deep sky. Who knows its exquisite color?

Wind and dust, one calamity after another. And no letters
across frontier passes all isolate silence, roads impossible.

After ten years of wandering desperation, driven from this
frail perch to that, I cling to what peace a lone twig holds.

Sleepless Night

Bamboo chill drifts far into sleep. Wildland
moonlight fills our courtyard's every corner.

Heavy dew beads and trickles. Sparse stars
kindle Presence—then darken into Absence.

Fireflies in dark flight *flash*, *flash*. Lingering
night out on water, birds call back and forth.

All things caught between shield and sword,
all grief empty—the clear night passes away.

Setting Out by Boat

We furl sails and head down wild water,
roll up canopies through seething rapids,

river markets busy in battle-tribe shadow.
Mountain clouds billow murky and cold,

forests vast tangles, not a path anywhere.
A lone bird scolds me for looking. Then

we settle at anchor beneath a wall-tower.
How will night's darkness ever end here?

SOUTH: TRIPLE-GORGE

(765–768)

AFTER A SIX-MONTH pause along the river in Cloud-Poise because of a deterioration in his health, Tu Fu found refuge with his family at Ample-Awe City. Ample-Awe was located at the head of Triple-Gorge, a two-hundred-mile series of spectacular gorges formed where the Yangtze cuts through the Shamaness Mountains and legendary for the river's violence beneath towering cliffs alive with shrieking gibbons. Tu was now on the very outskirts of Chinese civilization. Although traces of his culture reached towns along the river, the region was populated by aboriginal tribes that spoke languages unintelligible to Tu Fu. Despite this disorienting situation, or perhaps because of it, this was Tu's most productive period: he wrote more than a quarter of his surviving poems during his three years there, among them poems that opened stark new dimensions of elemental experience.

Tu Fu first rented a house outside the city, where he struggled to make ends meet. Eventually, he found a patron in the local prefect, who provided him with a token job in his administration and living quarters atop a tower above the city-wall. While his family continued to live in the rented farmhouse outside the city, Tu stayed mostly at West Tower with its spectacular views of the gorge, deep skies, and the Shamaness Mountains out beyond. There, he was free of distractions and able to write with his full attention. After nine months in West Tower, Tu's poor health forced him to resign his position: it seems he developed diabetes, in addition to his ongoing asthma, malaria, and rheumatism. With his patron's parting gift, Tu was able to buy two farms outside the city, which he managed for a relatively happy year. But then, ever restless for home in the north, Tu left all that and sailed with his family through the breathtaking Triple-Gorge, then on downriver into China's far southlands.

Almost Dawn

City-wall clappers end the final watch.
Iron locks—gates ready to swing open.

Drums and horns grieving borderlands,
Star River cascades past dawn-lit peaks.

People here rebellious, imperial envoys
come and never return. My isolate old-

age-color sails laze and drift, trespassing
now into wild lands of a hundred tribes.

Brimmed Whole

River moon cast mere feet away, wind-lamps
alight late into the second watch . . . . Serene

flock of fists along sand—egrets asleep when
a fish leaps in the boat's wake, shivering, cry.

Bringing Water

Lumen-Moon Gorge and Fear-Wall: clouds mountaintops,
a confusion of rock, peak, and summit. No place for wells.

In Cloud-Poise, my servants hated that we paid for water,
but that heartache's gone now we've come to Further-Fish

out west of Amble-Awe City. Ten thousand bamboo pipes
twist and turn, bringing water. No more dry throat for me.

Life waylaid and tangled: who sees the inner-pattern here?
But a ladle of water opens every worry so perfectly away.

For Little-Tale, My Tribal Servant

Mountain forests all deep-shadow greens, dusk smoky dark,
bamboo pipe twisted and swayed, breaking the delicate flow.

Neighbors went out into the night, bickered over last drops,
but our servant ignored it all, went straight up to the source,

and in the third watch, disease-thirst fierce, I heard it trickle,
turned my white head to see water from green-azure clouds.

Legend's Mongol servant once awed me, but you're always
amazing: breezing through tiger-and-panther packs like that.

My Friend Shows Me a Scroll of Chang Hsü's Calligraphy

This sage of cursive-script: he's dead now,
and his mysteries are impossible to fathom.

When my friend unfurls a scroll before me,
it fills my eyes with a single icy sympathy:

such grief-winds born of sparse gauze-silk
and ancient colors ten thousand miles risen,

such clittering of jade-pure bells crying out,
flocks of pine perfectly clear and scattering,

and ranged mountains coiled into writhing
sea depths heaving his brush on, boundless.

Scrawling raw silk before it's dyed for cloth,
pond black from all the brushes he cleaned,

he was chief among calligraphy's renowned,
opening in late years the far ends of thought.

In the hundred generations since those two
original masters, who has ever equaled this

essence of southeast spirit, this *ch'i*-power
wild and free tracing insight's purest clarity?

Sweeping dust from his cabinet, my friend
unrolls a scroll and we forget to eat or sleep,

pondering how a long-ago brush-tip soared,
how wine's wonder was only the beginning.

Amble-Awe, on the City-Wall's Highest Tower

Along a city-wall's peaked walkway, pennants and flags
grieve. I stand alone on this soaring mist-and-haze tower,

dragons and tigers asleep in the gorge's fog-drift depths,
tortoise and crocodile roaming a clear river cradling sun.

Solar-Origin Tree spread west to cut cliffs, River-Source
shadow flowing east to long rapids . . . Whose child am I

on this goosefoot cane, lamenting the world? I look away,
white-haired descendent of emptiness mourning parents.

Amble-Awe City

Above the city-wall at Amble-Awe, cloud-form villages.
Below, wind-tossed rain sheeting down, a swollen river

heaves in gorges. Thunder and lightning battle. Silvered
wisteria and kingfisher-green trees shroud sun and moon.

War horses are nothing like horses gone back to pasture,
but for every thousand homes, a scarce hundred remain.

Ai, ai—that lone widow beaten by life's toll, grief-torn,
sobbing in what village where out across autumn plains?

Overnight at the River Tower

Evening colors linger on mountain paths.
This library's perched above a river gate:

sparse cloud overnight along far clifftops,
lone moon buffeted into tumbling waves.

Cranes trail away in flight. Silence open,
wolves snarl over the kill. I'm sleepless,

brooding on war, and powerless to right
those ancient ways of Heaven and Earth.

Dusk Skies Clear

Dusk's failing flare breaks slanting through,
then clouds thin away and drift. None return.

River rainbow drinks radiant distances. Rain
sheets into gorges; remnants scatter into sky.

Ducks and cranes set out into depths of blue
everywhere. Well-fattened bears rest content.

Autumn equinox. Still a wanderer, still here:
Dew on bamboo. And twilight sparse, sparse.

Night

Autumn sky-*ch'i* clear, dew settles under towering heavens,
and in empty mountains, isolate nights startle my homeless

spirit away. Lone overnight sail, distant, lantern lit of itself.
New moon lingering. A fulling-stick cracks *once . . . twice.*

A man sick in bed, I meet southern chrysanthemums again.
Heartless geese never bringing letters from the north, I pace

leaning on a cane beneath eaves. Herdboy, Northern Dipper,
Star River spread far, far: it must reach that ravaged capital.

Firewood-Carry Chant

Amble-Awe women, their hair turned half silvered-white:
forty years old, or fifty, and still not sold into some man's

home. No market for brides in this relentless ruin of war,
they live one long lament, nothing but sorrow to embrace.

Here, a tradition of men sitting keeps women on the run:
men sit inside doors and gates; women bustle in and out,

and returning home, eight or nine in ten carry firewood
on their backs, firewood they sell to keep families alive.

Old as they are, they keep their hair in twin virgin-knots,
silver hairpins holding mountain leaves and wildflowers,

and if not struggling precariously up toward market gates,
they ravage themselves working salt mines for a pittance.

Adorned in makeup and jewelry, shambles of teary sobs
and cold clothes among cliff-roots: *frightful things*, they

call these Shamaness Mountain women. So how is it she
came from a village so near: Lumen-Regal, sheer beauty?

Full Moon

Above the tower, a twice-sized moon drifts
alone. It passes night-filled homes on a cold

river, scattering restless golds across waves,
kindles mats, ignites gauze window-screens.

Flawless in the silence of empty mountains,
floating high among scarce stars, it finds my

far-off garden: pine, cinnamon. All light, all
ten thousand miles radiance at once in light.

Past Midnight

Out on West Tower, a thousand feet up,
I wander by gauze window-screens past

midnight. Falling stars flare on the river.
Low moon wavers on river sand, empty.

Birds are known by woods they choose,
great fish by their hermit deeps. Those I

love fill all Heaven and Earth—but still,
shield and sword make even letters rare.

Bridal-Chamber

Bridal-chamber waist-jewels ice-cold,
autumn wind scours royal halls of jade.

This new moon must drift there, capital
where palaces founder in Dragon Lake,

and distances tether boats here tonight.
Clepsydra drops lucid as ever, all ruins

ten thousand miles north of Yellow Peak:
imperial tombs in a lake of white frost.

Autumn Thoughts

1

Jade-pure frost wilts and wounds maple trees, wind-scoured
Shamaness Mountain forests rising from Shamaness Gorge,

ch'i-sky deep. River billows and swells breach sky churning,
and clouds blown over frontier passes touch shadow to earth.

Chrysanthemum thickets have opened tears here twice—my
lost lives, my lone boat moored to a homesick heart. Winter

clothes: everywhere cloth's cut urgently to pattern, and high
above city-walls, fulling-stone rhythms tighten into twilight.

2

Each night, slant light of dusk leaving Amble-Awe, isolate city,
I find the Northern Dipper and gaze toward our radiant capital.

It's true of gibbon voices here: *three cries, and you're in tears.*
Appointed to an empty journey on that Star River raft, far from

palace incense and stately portraits, I lie sick among mountain
towers and whitewashed battlements. One hidden flute mourns,

and look, look there amid cliffwall wisteria, the moon: already,
all along island shallows, in blossoms atop silver-grass it flares!

3

Silence, this mountain city of a thousand houses: I sit radiant
morning after morning in a river tower, face distant kingfisher-

greens, sparse. After two nights, fishermen drifting home drift.
Crystalline autumn keeps swallows urgent in headlong flight.

We're far from ancient times: sage advice to emperors earns
scant honor now, and who dreams of teaching wisdom books?

Wealth eluded few of my classmates: fine clothes and horses
out light and sleek where those five noble heroes lie in tombs.

4

They say our capital's like a besiege-chess board. Grief remains
unconquered, even after a century of bitter struggle everywhere.

Fledgling lords have moved into all those stately mansions now,
new scholars and generals flaunting caps and robes replace old,

as gongs and drums cry war through mountain borderlands north.
Armies trundle westward: horses, carts. Feathered messages fly.

Autumn river cold, dragons and fish all isolate silence. It's our
quiet, long-ago country: that's what keeps haunting my thoughts.

5

The palace's Immortality Land gates face South Mountain.
Gold stalks stand gathering long-life dew in the Star River.

Goddess Queen-Mother soars east to Jasper Lake, *ch'i*-mist
drifts west with Lao Tzu, purple across Sheath-Ravine Pass.

Palace screens open, pheasant-tail plumage clears cloud,
sun-wreathed dragon scales: our sage emperor appears and . . .

A single sleep, this vast river startled by year's end—I was
there how many dawns, imperial gates jewel-azure flaring?

6

From this Fear-Wall Gorge to the capital's Meandering River,
ten thousand miles of smoke-scored wind weave silvered-silk

autumn together. Regal *ch'i*-presence—the emperor wanders
Calyx Tower arcade, frontier grief pouring into Hibiscus Park.

Pearl screens and embroidered columns nestle yellow herons
where white gulls scatter off brocade rigging and ivory masts:

I turn toward it, ancient land of song and dance, turn and pity
our northland home to heaven's emperors from the beginning.

7

The capital's Bright-Posterity Lake, Han Dynasty masterwork:
I can see the warrior emperor's banners and flags billowed out

and Weaver-Girl, her loom of origins casting empty moonlight,
facing a jade whale. Its armor scales shudder in autumn wind,

seeds of wave-tossed orphan-rice drowned in pitch-dark cloud,
and icy frost sending rouge-powder sifting off lotus seed-pods.

Frontier passes teeter into deepest sky. Only birds can make it
through. Here in this land of rivers and lakes: a lone fisherman.

8

Our-Posterity Road wanders Regal-Overnight Creek at home
in capital outlands, Beauty-Swell Lake in Purple-Tower Peak

shadow. Fragrant field-rice warrior-bird grains, pecked-over
remains. In emerald kindred-trees aging perch emperor-birds,

as exquisite women gather kingfisher-green springtime gifts
and immortals set out again in their boat. It is late. My florid

brush once defied the *ch'i*-shape of things: now I gaze mirror-
deep into wildlands—hair white, gaze grief-sung and sinking.

After a Night at West Tower, Dawn

Night-watches pass quickly in city dark.
Rain and snow in these tower heights thin,

bare hints through silk curtains, and then
clear skies. Far off, Jade-String stars sink.

Dawn's blaze startles magpies at the gate,
and crows on yardarms lunge into flight.

Cold river scarcely moves, gossamer *ch'i*-
thoughts of those waiting to return home.

Night at the Tower

Yin and *yang* cut brief autumn days short. Frost and snow
clear, leaving cold night wide-open at the edge of heaven.

Marking the fifth watch, grieving drums and horns erupt.
Star River, shadows trembling, drifts Triple-Gorge depths.

War's pastoral weeping filling homes far and wide, tribal
woodcutters and fishermen trail wild song here into skies.

Slumber-Dragon, Leap-Stallion: all dark earth in the end.
And the story of our lives just opens away—vacant, silent.

Fear-Wall Gorge Cliffs

People may not call this part of Triple-Gorge,
but the facing cliffs shape a magisterial gate

towering deep into sky and still seeming rock,
piercing this river through sudden cloud-root

amid yellow-beard gibbon ancients, venerable
flood-dragon dens. O great Sun-Mother, your

six-dragon sun-carriage along winter clifftops:
it might catch and come crashing down here!

Soaking Up Sun at West Tower

Tired of dark-enigma's icy winter, I adore
this soaring tower. I lie bare-backed here,

and Sun-Mother's nobility nourishes me.
Shaming that miserly god of winter, she

kindles every last hair back to life again,
secretly enriching skin deep into muscle.

Vast Solar-*Yang*, her open-hearted depths
suddenly nurturing my age-ravaged *ch'i*,

tipped askew, pouring clear through sight
and so easily restoring these diseased feet.

Vagabond gibbons haunt treetops out here.
Fluttering cranes dance on mountain peaks.

Friends in sorrow gathering and scattering,
day after day such tangles of joy and grief:

this life becoming so suddenly yesterdays,
I only make poems of whatever I'm facing.

Facing ravaged times since deep antiquity,
sage-masters realized isolate silence whole:

where am I, not yet far into twilight years,
heart and mind already too frail for all that?

Bound-Chickens Chant

Our young servant's bound the chickens to sell at market,
and the bound chickens thrash around, squawk and shriek.

My family hates how the chickens eat insects and beetles,
but don't they know sold chickens get cooked for dinner?

And how can we say which matters most, chicken or bug?
So I shout for the servant to set them free. Chicken or bug,

life or death—it never ends. My refuge this mountain hut,
I gaze out at the cold river, and it's inside my eyes flowing.

River Plums

Buds breaking at winter-solstice festival,
plums lavish the new year with countless

blossoms. *Ch'i*-mind spring means well,
but who could bear this wanderer's grief?

At origins, snow and tree share one color,
it's true, river and wind one wave. Still—

I can't see my old gardens, just skylines
erratic with Shamaness Mountain peaks.

Southland

Spring green is a marvel in this southland,
and the break from cold to warm so early.

River grass free of names. Cloud unfurling
ch'i-mind on mountain peaks. First moon:

already bees everywhere, and birdsong all
out of season. It's this old goosefoot cane

keeps me from frolicking like antic ponies,
not loneliness for good company far away.

Late Spring

I lie ill beside gorges, shut-in. Far-off Goddess-Court Lake,
rivers Gossamer and Appearance all empty mirage of sunlit

emptiness now . . . . Skies here rain year-round. And winds,
ten-thousand-mile Shamaness Gorge winds: they never end.

Here at my thatch hut out beyond city-walls, fresh shadows
fill riverbank willows, the pond's lotus blossoms hint at red:

it's late spring. Ducks and egrets stand along island shallows,
chicks nestled in among them, fluttering off, quick to return.

Here, This Moment

Late spring, the third month—Shamaness Gorges stretch on:
clouds incandescent white wandering, drifting solar radiance,

and thunder suddenly sending rain across a thousand peaks.
Blossom-*ch'i* a confusion thick as Hundred-Accord incense,

yellow orioles come crossing the river, then fly back across.
Swallows carry mud in their beaks, unconcerned with mists.

I raise blinds in this soaring tower, and I'm in a painting: all
empty Absence, those southland river-distances missing too.

Moving into the New House

Cragged Crimson-Scale heaved up behind,
White-Salt cliffwall chiseled clean in front:

a wanderer's helpless against moving often,
but spring beauty steadily flares, blossoms

smothering bamboo starts we'll transplant,
and once we raise the blinds, birds peer in.

How could I resent the ruins of age? Here
I've found this sheer wonder's become me.

Late Spring, Inscribed on a Wall at the House We Just Leased in Highwater West

I

So long a wanderer in lament, I meet
late spring again at Triple-Gorge, its

hundred tongues nearing silence. This
onslaught of blossoms can't last, now

ch'i-haze thins over valley emptiness
and majestic sun drifts battered wave.

Where can war's end begin? Wounded
grief is nowhere in all this—nowhere.

3

Flaring cloud smolders dark, then white.
Brocade trees azure-green, dawn comes,

this world and I a braid of bramble-hair,
all Heaven and Earth a single thatch-hut.

Wounded song welcoming my failings, I
dance drunk. Who needs me sober? Rain

slight, I shoulder my hoe. River gibbons
cry out cliffs a kingfisher-green painting.

Morning Rain

A slight rain comes, bathed in dawn light.
I hear it among treetop leaves before mist

arrives. It sprinkles soil then scatters wind-
lashed, following clouds away. Deepened

purples flare across thorn-bramble houses,
flocks and herds of things wild glistening

faintly. Then scents of musk open across
half a mountain, and linger on past noon.

Failing Flare

North of an ancient emperor's palace, dusk burns yellow.
Traces of rain drift west of Amble-Awe city-walls. Soon,

day's failing flare kindles river, roils across cliffs. Then
returning clouds muffle forests, erase mountain villages.

Lungs sick, ruins of age, I rest propped high on pillows,
and these borderlands impenetrable, close my gate early.

How long can I survive these tiger-and-wolf calamities,
and no home left to summon my far-off spirit for burial?

The Houseboy Comes

Emerald greens only tinge haw and pear
now. Apricot and plum shine half yellow.

From orchards of quiet mystery, the boy
comes bringing fruit in delicate baskets:

ripe, fragrant, fresh flavors replete with
mountain wind and iced with wild frost.

Sick in bed, a guest of rivers and lakes, I
linger out days and months in each taste.

Getting Free of Sorrow

I nurture simplicity, my door mere bramble
opening onto what boundless and beyond?

River far as that goddess's mountain palace,
no Gaze-Homeward Terrace anywhere near,

resentment over my age-ruined face grows,
and how can I bring brother and sister here?

Sword and spear, those grand human affairs:
turn, look away, and it's all one single grief.

Watching Fireflies

In autumnal Shamaness Mountain night, fireflies in flight
meander auspiciously through open-weave blinds, light on

my robes. It startles me: the whole room, books and *ch'in*,
suddenly cold. Out beyond eaves, erratic, they tangle thin

stars, wander over well-pond rails, adding to each another
light, happen past blossoms, color flashing: *here . . . there.*

River vast, hair white—I watch grief-stricken, study what
you know: on this day next year, will I be home, will I not?

Our Field Inspector Returns Home After Checking Irrigation for the Rice Fields

North of the great river, my east-village
land spreads flat as a table, fifteen acres

azure-green rice lavish this sixth month,
a thousand fields wild emerald streams.

Once we'd transplanted the sprouts out,
we diverted water down to flood fields,

sent other servants out to the reservoirs
where they cleared out ditches on slopes,

so public and private lands alike flourish,
well-flooded and safe from rainless skies.

When the inspector visited village elders,
he could see field paths, rice still flaring

dense and lush, kingfisher-green feathers,
Star River speckled shimmering of sparks

in this mirror gulls come soaring through
boundary mountains edging up into cloud.

In autumn, wild rice ripens shadow-black,
and white alight by the radiant basketful,

jade grains we'll steam pure for breakfast,
and red scattered fresh like dusk-lit cloud.

Finally, this wanderer will riot in enough
food. It's bitter work, but a splendid sight,

and plenty left in the fields for gleaners!
Don't stuff our granary too awfully full!

After Three or Four Years of Silence, No News from My Fifth Brother Who Is Living Alone on the East Coast South of the River, I Search for Someone Who Might Carry This to Him

I hear you've found mountain-monastery
refuge in far River-Ford or Beyond-Land.

Dust and wind: war drags out separation,
autumn clarity passes unnoticed. Shadow

rooted here in gibbon-shriek forests, my
spirit buffets away to mirage sea-towers.

Next spring, I'll sail flood-waters, search
all the way east, white cloud and beyond.

Opening Depression Away

1

Thatch hut, brushwood gate: stars scatter to shelter.
Waves churn black river. Soon, rainfall starts flying.

A mountain bird leads chicks to dine on red berries.
A girl at the stream takes a coin, leaves a white fish.

12

It grows far off, isolate up wild slopes, along riverbanks,
won't ripen in jade pots at cinnabar palaces. Cloud-valley

folk in rags, blowfish-backed: they die gathering lychee,
horses ravaged, all to pamper kingfisher-green eyebrows.

Lone Goose

Lone goose in flight never eats or drinks,
just calls out longing for its flock. Who

pities it—a flake of shadow lost beyond
ten thousand billows of cloud? It stares

far off, as if glimpses of them remained.
Sorrows mount: it can almost hear them.

Their *ch'i*-thought all unraveled, crows
squawk and shriek confusions of scatter.

Taking the Day Off, Trying to Ease My Sickness in the Small Garden, Preparing to Plant Fall Vegetables and Directing the Plow-Ox: Writing Whatever My Eye Encounters

I don't like being in Amble-Awe City,
the ways people there suspect honest

simplicity, but back home here at this
thatch hut, neighbors never complain,

and even tangled in age and sickness,
worry over things ravaging my spirit,

my river-village mind drifts effortless
and free, this forest my heart's delight.

Autumn plowing depends on wet soil,
and mountain rains have been steady:

this winter, leeks will be half our food.
Farm-ox grown stronger at year's end,

I plow deeply, plant a few fresh acres.
We're not so far behind our neighbors.

With so many kinds of tasty vegetables,
we label them all, and it's never bitter

cold in this Thorn-Bramble Shamaness
land: we'll pick clear through to spring.

A pair of white cranes comes gliding in,
pecks at celery seed in the mud at dusk:

the male's left wing hangs, wreckage
wounded deep, muscles left out bare,

and with each step fresh blood surges.
Still struggling against that bird-arrow,

it cries out six times every three steps,
urgent and pleading, hopelessly grief-

stricken. No phoenix waiting, its neck
twisted, it complains to autumn skies.

Goosefoot cane, gazing at sandy isles,
I'm with you, nostrils stung in anguish.

Musk Deer

Losing clear streams forever, you'll end
served up like jade dainties. How could

you master the recluse life of immortals,
you, unable even to resent fine kitchens?

Once times fall apart, anything's a trifle,
sparse voice at disaster's heart, anything.

Noblemen noble as thieves, gluttonous,
you'll get wolfed down in a royal trice.

Our Thatch Hut

Our thatch hut perched where land ends,
I leave my brushwood gate open always.

Dragons and fish settled into dark waters,
moon and stars drift autumn peaks. Frost

gathers clarity, then trickles. High clouds
thin away—none return. Girls man wind-

tossed boats at anchor—young, ashamed,
that river life battering their warm beauty.

Autumn Clarity

Now high autumn's clearing my lung-*ch'i*,
I can comb this white hair myself. Sick of

drug-cakes—always a bit more, a bit less—
I struggle to sweep courtyard and gate-path,

lean on a goosefoot cane to welcome guests.
And I leave poems adoring bamboo to kids.

Come winter, river steady and smooth again,
a light boat will carry me anywhere I please.

8th Moon, 17th Night: Facing the Moon

The autumn moon is still round tonight.
In this river village, isolate old wanderer

hoisting blinds, I return to its brilliance,
and propped on a cane, follow it further:

radiance rousing hidden dragons, bright
scatters of birds aflutter. Thatched study

incandescent, I trust to this orange grove
ablaze: clear dew aching with fresh light.

Dawn Landscape

The last watch has sounded in Amble-Awe.
Radiant color spreads above Solar-Terrace

Mountain, then cold sun clears high peaks.
Mist and cloud linger across layered ridges,

and earth split-open hides river sails deep.
Leaves clatter at heaven's clarity. I listen,

and face deer at my bramble gate: so close
here, we touch our own kind in each other.

Day's End

Oxen and sheep come back down long ago,
brushwood gates closed, a windswept moon

rises into its own clear night, my old garden
nowhere among these rivers and mountains.

Crag-rock springs cascade down dark cliffs.
Frost infuses autumn-grass distances. White

hair is radiant by lamplight, but why assume
its flame flickering out foretells dark trouble?

9th Moon, 1st Sun: Visiting Friends

My goosefoot cane invades frost. Dawn
light trailed out on bramble-gate smoke,

I stop for rest beneath every tree I pass:
old, frail, dozing among books my limit.

Autumn ends whatever once drove me:
nothing but your friendship could bring

me here. Flavors rich in your small talk
crystal clear, I forget all those years lost.

I Rely on a Friend to Take a Letter North and Search Out My Old Family Farm at Land-Tower

Scatter and confusion ended, I live at peace
here. Far from All-Water Brights pinnacles,

never leaving thorn-bramble depths of home,
I ponder the question cloud-lost peaks pose.

Yellow leaves tumble away on north winds.
Southern streams extract white-hair lament.

Ten years amid rivers and lakes, boundless,
this mind all lingering dusk—it's boundless.

Climbing Tower Heights

Skies bottomless, gibbon howls tear through gusting wind.
White sand, clear shallows: birds scatter, then birds return.

Hissing through trees, wind tumbles leaves boundless away,
while the Yangtze, one headlong crash, arrives without end.

I've wandered forever in autumn's ten-thousand-mile grief,
a lifetime rife with sickness, but here today I climb a tower

and stand alone. Hair all frost bitter trouble and worry bring,
defeated . . . and I've just sworn it off, wine thick and fresh?

Autumn Wildlands

Autumn wildlands sun-desolate, a cold
river jostling sky's jade-pure emptiness,

I tied my boat to Well-Rope, aboriginal
star, *ch'i*-sited a house in empty village

southlands. Workers pick ripened dates,
but I hoe my sunflower wreckage alone,

and dinners the food of old-timers now:
I share them out mid-stream among fish.

2

It's easy to find the inner-pattern of this
drifting life. Nothing ever turns against it:

fish are happiest in deep waters, and birds
feel most at home where forests are thick.

Feeble and old, I'm content sick and poor:
life's pageant flares good and bad together.

Autumn wind, cane, pillow: I never tire of
North Mountain's bitter thorn-bean flavors.

3

Music and ritual perfect imperfection, sage
masters say, mountains and forests enduring

joy, but leaving my gauze cap fallen askew,
I sun in the radiance of bamboo and books,

gather wind-scattered pinecones, slice sky-
chilled honeycomb open. In clumsy shoes,

I wander flecks of red and kingfisher-blue,
pausing to lean in toward faint fragrances.

4

Autumn sand white out along far shores,
dusk light kindles mountains red nearby.

Hidden scales churn up terrifying waves.
High in wind, wings gather toward return,

as fulling-stones echo house after house,
and axe-strokes *crack*, *crack*. The winter

goddess sends frost flying, quilt blessing
come between me and South Palace stars.

5

I wanted to rescue it all, win Dragon-Horse
honor. Now amid flocks of duck and egret,

my years crumble. Autumn floods this vast
river, night sounds haunting empty gorges.

Paths lost in thousand-layer cliffs, our sail
lingers on, a single flake of cloud. My sons:

though well-versed in tribal speech, glory
advising fine generals isn't likely for them.

I Send Servant Boys to Clear Brush and Prune the Fruit Orchard North of Our House, Where Branches and Vines Sprawled into Wild Tangles. Then, When It's All Cleaned Up, They Carry My Bed Out There

As I lie sick beneath thatched beams,
blades clean out our tangled orchard,

then, home behind me, distances open,
wildland thought gone clear and deep.

Mountain pheasants fend off intruders.
River gibbons answer chanted poems,

and high clouds laze, going nowhere.
Quiet in secret, I'm pure no-mind too.

Asking Again

Couldn't we just let her filch dates from the garden?
She's a neighbor, childless and without food, alone:

only desperation would bring her to this. We should
treat her like family. It will ease her fear and shame.

She knows us now, but strangers from far away still
frighten her. A fence would only make things worse.

Tax collectors hound her, she says, keeping her bone
poor. How suddenly war rifles thought, leaving tears.

East Village, North Mountain

Rebel bandits gave me this drifting life.
Tax collectors keep simple people poor,

these villages empty: nothing but birds.
I haven't met anyone all day. At sunset,

I wander along the ravine, facing wind,
gaze at pines, frost scattered across me.

Head white, I turn toward distant peaks,
but find battlefields full of yellow dust.

Gone Deaf

I'm old as ancient Master Pheasant-Cap,
lament this world like Elder Deer-Skin:

how long before darkness fills my eyes?
For over a month now, deaf as dragons:

autumn tears absent when gibbons howl,
old-age grief empty when sparrows cry.

Yellow falling, mountain trees startle me.
I call out to my son: *Is there north wind?*

Rain

Rain too sparse to set roads glistening,
broken clouds thin away. Come again

in a rush, they swell purple cliffs black,
harry white birds into distances radiant,

and soon dampen autumn-sun shadow,
clatter ancient rain across a cold river.

Below our brushwood gate, at the mill:
hulled plain-rice, half-wet and fragrant.

Facing Night

In farmland outside a lone city, our river
village inhabits streamwater confusions.

Deep mountains hurry brief winter light
here, lofty trees at ease high amid winds.

Cranes glide down, touch cloud shallows.
Sharing our thatch hut, chickens settle-in.

All night long, books and *ch'in* scattered
candlelight—I can see through my death.

Rice Cut and Gather Chant

The rice harvest empties water to cloud.
A glassy river mirrors stone-gate cliffs.

Cold wind clearing fieldgrass and trees,
dawn light scattering chickens and pigs,

wildland sobbing begins, sound of war,
and woodcutter song leaves the village.

No home for news, I wander still, trust
myself to powers of Heaven and Earth.

Dusk's Failing Flare

Dusk's failing flare opens Shamaness Gorge,
icy sky emptiness of Presence half Absence.

Fish hidden low return to swelling darkness.
White-Salt's clifftop towering alone, still lit.

Silver-grass shores move like autumn water,
and pine gates here: they could be paintings.

Oxen and sheep know our herdboy: tonight
they'll call out, teach him essential doctrine.

Morning

Dawn clear south of the southland palace,
frosty sky holds ten thousand peaks in its

emptiness. I sometimes wander off alone.
Wildland cloud blurring lit trees together,

a majestic hawk slips by without a sound,
hungry crows plummet and feed greedily.

In the end, this sick body will stop moving.
Leaves just tumble down into a river pool.

Night

1

Flutes mourn out on city-walls at dusk.
Last birds cross our village graveyard,

and after years of battle, their war-tax
taken, people walk home in deep night.

Trees dark against cliffs scatter leaves,
and Star River, sparse, skirts frontiers.

The Dipper tilts away. I watch, watch.
Thin moon. Magpies finish with flight.

2

A sliver of moon lulls through clear night.
Half abandoned to sleep, lampwicks char.

Deer roam, uneasy among howling peaks,
and falling leaves startle locusts. Suddenly,

I remember mince treats east of the river,
and that boat drifting through falling snow.

Tribal song trails out, rifling the stars. Here
at the edge of heaven, I inhabit my absence.

Visiting the Ch'an Master at Clarity-Absolute Monastery

Isolate, high among mountain peaks rising
ridge beyond ridge, dawn smoldering mist,

icy stream spread thin across a gravel bed,
sunlit snow tumbling from towering pines:

in such dharma perfected, poems are folly.
And I am who I am, lazy even about wine,

so how could I renounce wife and children,
ch'i-site home again beneath further peaks?

Thoughts

Through all Heaven and Earth, everything
alive contends. It's like this anywhere, this

headlong wrangle forever among ourselves,
tangling ourselves ever tighter in the snare.

If nothing's treasured, nothing's worthless,
erase wealth, and poverty's plenty enough,

but ten thousand ages are one single corpse:
neighborhoods just take turns with lament.

I've lived a vagabond in Shamaness Gorge
three unkempt years like a guttering candle:

luckily I've grown content in failure by now,
and forgotten how honor and disgrace differ.

Cozy at court or grown old in some outland,
I need the same rice, and here at my bramble-

weave house east of city-walls, I can gather
healing herbs in shadowy mountain valleys,

and mind inhabiting frost and snow depths,
I never think about lush vines and orchards.

It isn't some discipline. It's just what I am,
this life in lone accord with quiet mystery.

They say a great sage is taut as a bowstring,
a dullard bent hookwise. Who knows which

I am? Taut hookwise, warming my old back
in sun, I wait out woodcutters and shepherds.

2

I sit on our south porch in deep night,
moonlight incandescent on my knees,

gusty winds tumbling Star River away
until morning sun clears the rooftops.

Things wild sleep alone. Then waking,
they set out in herds and flocks. And I

too hurry kids along, scratch out our
living with the same stingy industry.

Passersby grow rare under cold year-
end skies. Suns and moons slip away.

Caught in the scramble for glory, we
people made bedlam lice of ourselves.

Before the Three Emperors, people ate
and were content, then someone began

knotting ropes, and now we're mired
in the glue and varnish of government.

It began in Brush-Flame, finder of fire,
and Lead-Right's histories made it pure

disaster. If you light candles and lamps,
you know moths will gather in swarms.

Search out through all eight horizons:
you find nothing anywhere but isolate

emptiness of departure and return one
movement, one ageless way of absence.

Yin-Dark Again

Dark-enigma winter bleeds through dark-enigma's *yin*-dark
frontiers. Yesterday, skies cleared late. Today, they're black,

lit thistledown blown ten thousand dusk-flared miles
across.
On a lone city-wall, feathered war-flags trail out downwind.

River-swells rake across shorelines, tear yellow sand away.
Cloud and snow bury mountains. A wild silver-ash ox roars.

Has no one seen,
come so far from that Tu family village to these southlands,
this old-timer: teeth half fallen out, left ear deaf as dragons?

Returning Late

Past midnight, eluding tigers on the road, I return
home in mountain darkness. Family asleep inside,

I watch the Northern Dipper drift low to the river,
and Venus lofting huge into empty space, radiant.

Holding a candle in the courtyard, I call for more
light. A gibbon in the gorge, startled, shrieks once.

Old and tired, my hair white, I dance and sing out:
goosefoot cane, no sleep . . . *Catch me if you can!*

SOUTH: LAST POEMS

(768–770)

HOME FOR TU FU was in the north: the capital, the family farm he still owned in his ancestral village just south of the capital, and an estate his family owned further east. Tu Fu hoped was to sail down the Yangtze River, then travel up the Han River and continue overland back home to the capital. Traveling down the river, he found the devastation of war widespread there too, speaking in one untranslated poem of wolves and tigers prowling deserted river villages. Hearing of yet another Tibetan invasion in the capital region, Tu abandoned his plan to return north and sailed south across Goddess-Court Lake, hoping to find assistance from friends and relatives along Appearance River south of the lake. Tu and his family found help here and there, but their respites from poverty were brief. At times there was so little food they had to ration it. They fled a local rebellion, disguising themselves as peasants and passing dead bodies rotting on the roadside. Tu's ill health worsened. His wife, now in her forties, gave birth to a baby daughter, who died after only a year of life. Then, in the winter of 770, the family set out again for home in the north, and Tu Fu himself died on a boat sailing along the eastern shore of Goddess-Court Lake.

In the Great-Succession Reign's Third Year, I Leave Amble-Awe City, Setting Out by Boat Through Fear-Wall Gorge

Finally, grown old in Open-Hand country,
I leave this scrap of southern borderland,

though delight falters at the boat, my sigh
long and isolate as we cast off. And soon,

narrows twist depths, black apes howling:
we follow that emptiness, ducks startling,

mossy rock slipping past my unused cane,
kingfisher-green sky empty buffeting skin.

Cliffs parade layers of frost-edged sword,
streams cascading pearls of falling water,

and vines above plummet into dark deeps,
forests lavish and sparse, living and dying.

Goddess Peak exquisite, such lovely grace
(was that exiled beauty's home really here,

her song illuminating grief-stricken regret,
imperial dreams of pleasure lost for good),

we tumble on through seething whirlpools,
heaving waves tugging and tipping us over.

Wind and thunder pulse earth dragon-veins,
ice and snow mirror shimmering Star River,

and we careen through rapids at Deer Horn,
then Wolf Head blind in sheer recklessness:

so why blanch in fear of menacing shoals?
Indifferent to this sparse thing I am, I rest

at ease. Books and histories spilling loose,
baggage half-soaked and smashed on these

shorelines of life: I've faced the worst again,
but for the moment elude that place I'll die.

I only see the rampage those canyons were
when the river opens wide into level calm:

here, seas of mist flood Heaven and Earth,
dew and rain bathing wildgrasses of spring,

and gulls on silk puppet-thread buffet in air,
ashen dragons writhing, bathed in brocade

as dusk-lit cloud sinks into its green gauze,
a derelict moon ravaging its dark horizons.

Silver-grass young in bamboo-shoot mud,
tiny rushes pushing up through sand-grass,

baby ducks wrangle with shoreline horses,
and swallows scatter yardarm crows away.

Fog and mist billow across isolate islands,
nestled islands full glare of dusk and dawn,

and from Kiln-Hut pasturelands of legend
I turn, my gaze sweeping past Accord City,

imperial lands outside city-walls exquisite.
Then alone at a river crossing, I look north,

but now my stricken heart's grown serene.
Chanting this song—I'm lit with joy, *ch'i-*

mind free, all laughter. A ruins of old age,
I confuse wise and foolish, just laze wind-

drifted, sinking and floating, silvered hair
welcome. Let Great-Forge do what it will.

.   .   .

Traveling at Night

In delicate beach-grass, a slight breeze.
Boat masts teetering far up into isolate

night, stars founder across open plains.
Moon swells up flowing on a vast river.

How could poems bring honor? Career
lost into age and sickness, I soar wind-

drifted. Is there anything like it: endless
Heaven and Earth, and a lone sand-gull?

Riverside Moon and Stars

The sudden storm's left a clear, autumnal
night and Jade-String stars radiant in gold

waves. Star River lucent with beginnings:
its clarity claims Yangtze shallows afresh.

Strung-Pearls snaps, scattering shimmering
reflections. A mirror lofts into blank origin-

space. Of light, a clepsydra's remnant drop,
what remains with frost seizing blossoms?

Opposite a Post-Station, My Boat Moonlit Beside a Monastery

The boat mirroring crystalline moonlight
deep into the night, I leave candles unlit.

Golden monastery beyond green maples,
crimson post-tower beside lucent water:

faint, drifting from the city, a crow's cry
fades. Full of wild grace, egrets drowse.

Hair lit white, guest of rivers and lakes,
I tie blinds open and sit alone, sleepless.

Southland River-Country

I wander river-country dreaming return,
savant useless among Heaven and Earth:

sky shares my distances, flake of cloud,
and endless nights, a moon my solitude.

My heart grows strong still at sundown,
and in autumn wind, I am nearly healed:

didn't ancients always shelter old horses,
not send them off down such long roads?

Far Corner of Earth

River-country mountains loom, impassable.
Far corner of earth, windblown cloud adrift:

year after year, nothing's familiar. Nothing
anywhere but some further end of the line.

Poets both north and south found cold grief
out here, loss and confusion. My whole life

spent spirit-wounded—and now, I wander
every day a more profligate waste of road.

Leaving Equal-Peace at Dawn

In town to the north, the watchman's final clapper
falls silent again. Venus slipping away in the east,

neighborhood roosters mourn—same as yesterday.
How long can life's own sights and sounds endure?

My oar-strokes hushed, I leave for rivers and lakes,
distances without promise. I step out the gate, look

away, and all trace has vanished. These drug-cakes
shoring-up this tired life—they alone stay with me.

Year-End Chant

And so the year ends: north wind, white snow shrouding
this land of rivers and lakes: Gossamer and Appearance,

Goddess-Court. Fishermen tend frozen nets here beneath
cold skies, and tribesmen hunt geese with mulberry bows

loud at the shot. But southland people eat fish, not birds.
Let geese keep flying south: it's useless killing them here.

The price of rice soared last year, and our soldiers starved.
This year prices tumbled rock-bottom, ravaging farmers,

and grand officials ride high, stuffed with wine and meat,
while the looms in these fleeced thatch-huts stand empty.

I've even heard children are sold now, that it's common
everywhere: love hacked and smothered to pay out taxes.

They once jailed people for minting coin. But these days,
cutting green copper with iron and lead is approved. Why

bother? Engraved mud would be simpler. True and false
surely differ, but they've been blurred together for years,

and from city-walls of ten thousand lands, painted horns
cry war. Such sad anthems: when will they ever just end?

Deep Winter

Heaven's *ch'i*-mind blossoms and leafs
out. River and stream share stone roots.

Dawn-lit cloud mirroring shadow-glints,
cold currents trace along one scar. A lost

sage came to tears easily here, and who
could ever call that drowned poet back?

Waves billowing into teetering dusk: we
abandon oars for a night in whose home?

On Summit-Brights Tower

I've long heard of Goddess-Court Lake,
and today climb Summit-Brights Tower

there, prize distances east and west open,
Heaven and Earth adrift days and nights.

No more word from anyone I love. Old,
sick, nothing left now but this lone boat

and war-horses north of those mountain
frontiers: I clutch railing, and tears come.

Overnight at White-Sand
Post-Station

Another night on water: lingering light,
thatch-hut cook-smoke. Ancient white

sand beside a post-station. And beyond
this lake, fresh green wildgrass. Spring

ch'i: here among its ten thousand forms,
my isolate raft is another Wander Star.

Radiance following waves of moonlight
limitless, I shade into Southern Darkness.

Facing Snow

Northern snows overrun Long-Sand City,
Mongol stormclouds leaving ten thousand

homes cold. Buffeted among leaves, wind-
blown, it falls rain-smeared and flakeless.

Gold-stitched purse empty, my credit buys
silver-jar wine easily, its floating-ant dregs.

Absence alone for company, I'm Presence
itself awaiting dusk and the coming crows.

A Traveler From

A traveler from Southern Darkness came,
bringing a sea-goddess tear, perfect pearl

hiding at its center words mysterious and
half missing—words I couldn't decipher.

I packed it deep away long ago, savings
against those government clerks. Today,

opening fine wrappers, I find it turned to
blood, blood: nothing more left for taxes.

Silkworm and Grain Chant

Across all beneath heaven, all provinces and kingdoms,
there live ten thousand cities, and has any ever eluded

shield and sword? How is it weapons can't be cast into
ploughshares, and oxen till every inch of lost fieldland?

Tilled through by oxen,
fattened into silkworms . . .

Don't condemn warriors to weep heavy rains: leave our
men to grain, women to silk. Let us all go in song again.

Crossing Goddess-Court Lake

Azure-Grass Lake's dragon-den thickets,
White-Sand Post-Station at Dragon-Back

lost, and flood-dike trees in origin-times:
spirit-crows dance, welcoming oars, then

we're out fast on south winds, returning
home. I fear dusk light, but this dazzling

lake ranges into far heavens, and on this
Wander-Star raft, I'm sailing away there.

Lying Sick with Wind-Disease on a Boat, I Write Out My Thoughts in Thirty-Six Rhymes, Offer Them to Those I Love South of the Lake

Spare us this harmony you made of things.
Earth-Yellow, occurrence unhinged in your

squawking pipes; Provision-Sage, the very
heart of it all wounded in your dying *ch'in*:

what is your regal wisdom to this wanderer
caught here in these disease-ravaged years?

My boat still anchored along eastern shores,
I watch Orion rise early above a glassy lake,

listen grief-stricken to long-ago flute song
and hold robes open to cool northern winds.

I gaze toward ancient homelands brooding
and cold, the year blackened-over by cloud.

White houses vanishing in mist along water,
azure peaks ranged above maple shorelines,

it aches: winter's malarial fire aches. Grief
and these drizzling rains drizzle on and on,

drums welcoming ghosts never summoned
and crossbows slaughtering guardian owls.

When my spirits ebb away, I feel relieved.
And when grief comes, I let it come. I drift

shorelines of life, both sinking and floating,
occurrence now a perfect ruin of desertion.

·   ·   ·

NOTES

Biographical information in the section introductions is drawn from William Hung's *Tu Fu: China's Greatest Poet* (Cambridge: Harvard University Press, 1952).

13   *yin* and *yang*: The two fundamental forces of the universe: female and male, cold and hot, dark and light, earth and heaven. They arose from an undifferentiated primordial unity, and their interaction gives birth perennially to the empirical universe, its ten thousand things, and their constant transformations.

14   **Dragon:** Feared and revered as the awesome force of change, of life itself, the dragon in ancient China was a mythological embodiment of Tao and its ten thousand things tumbling through their traceless transformations. Small as a silkworm and vast as all heaven and earth, the dragon descends into deep waters in autumn, where it hibernates until spring, when its reawakening means the return of life to earth. It rises and ascends into sky, billowing into thunderclouds and falling as spring's life-bringing rains. Its claws flash as lightning in those thunderclouds, and its rippling scales glisten in the bark of rain-soaked pines.

15   **Inscribed on a Wall:** Inscribing poems on walls was common because calligraphy was high art—so, a poem enhanced by calligraphic art became a piece of visual art in a home.
Quiet mystery: See *Key Terms.*
ch'i: See *Key Terms.*
on a whim: The sage recluse Wang Hui-chih (d. 388 CE) set out "on a whim" to visit a friend. But when he arrived at the friend's house, the whim had vanished, so he simply returned home without seeing his friend. A famous example of everyday *wu-wei* action (see *Introduction,* p. 6).

20 This poem cycle was written in the voice of a commoner, a standard poetic practice that imitated folk poems, which were once collected by enlightened emperors so they could gauge the sentiments of their people in order to rule more effectively. Other examples can be found on pp. 57 and 74.

28 **resolute in privation**: From the *Analects* 15.2:
> In Ch'en, when supplies ran out, the disciples grew so weak they couldn't get to their feet. Adept Lu, his anger flaring, asked: "How is it the noble-minded must endure such privation?"
> "If you're noble-minded, you're resolute in privation," Confucius replied. "Little people get swept away."

29 **New Year's Eve**: In China's lunar year, New Year's comes a month or two after New Year's in the West, and it marks the beginning of spring. Traditionally, all Chinese people celebrated the lunar new year as their birthday, counting themselves a year older on that day.

30 **wine**: Drinking wine was generally seen as an aid in the practice of *wu-wei* (p. 6), wherein one moves with the effortless spontaneity of Tao's natural process. Indeed, the poet Po Chü-i said wine was the equal of Ch'an for enlightenment.
Meandering River: River flowing through a park lined with luxurious homes in the capital.

31 **9/9 Festival**: Dominated by thoughts of mortality, this autumn festival is celebrated on the ninth day of the ninth lunar month because the word for "nine" (*chiu*) is pronounced the same as the word meaning "long-lasting" or "long-living," hence, *9/9* sounds like "ever and ever." Hiking to mountaintops was a customary activity on this holiday, as was drinking chrysanthemum wine, which was playfully thought to promote long life.
South Mountain: Calling up such passages as "like the timelessness of South Mountain" in *The Book of Songs*, poets sometimes called local mountains "South Mountain" to suggest a kind of mythic stature as an embodiment of the elemental and timeless nature of the earth (cf. pp. 31, 35, 168, and the following note).

east fence ... chrysanthemums: The 9/9 Festival, wine, and yellow chrysanthemums at the east fence are famously associated with T'ao Ch'ien and allude to poems of his like this:

Drinking Wine

I live here in this busy village without
all that racket horses and carts stir up,

and you wonder how that could ever be.
Wherever the mind dwells apart is itself

a distant place. Picking chrysanthemums
at my east fence, I see South Mountain

far off: air lovely at dusk, birds in flight
going home. All this means something,

something absolute: whenever I start
to explain it, I forget words altogether.

34 **inner-pattern:** See *Key Terms.*

ch'in: Ancient stringed instrument much revered by Chinese intellectuals as a means for attaining enlightenment. Often appearing in poems, it was used as accompaniment when Chinese poets chanted their poems. In the hands of a master, a *ch'in* could voice with profound clarity the rivers-and-mountains realm, empty mind, even the very source of all things.

39 Fang Kuan, the general who led this Chinese army to such disastrous defeat, was a close friend of Tu Fu's and also a serious Ch'an practitioner. He and Tu Fu associated with the same group of Ch'an masters, including no less than one of the preeminent figures in the formation of Ch'an: Spirit-Lightning Wisdom (Shen Hui).

45   Here Tu is remembering a time just after rebel armies captured the capital, and he fled with his family north. He left them in Deer-Altar and attempted to rejoin the exile government, but somehow ended up hiding in the capital (see pp. 39–44).

46   **lure our distant spirits:** It was popularly believed that a spirit could leave the body when a person was asleep or frightened. Very different from the metaphysical "soul" of the West, the spirit in ancient China was something more earthly: a condensation of *ch'i*-energy that slowly faded away after death.

48   After a year assuming his family had been overrun by war, Tu learned that they were safe, and thereupon made the arduous journey from the exile capital (Phoenix-Soar) to join them. This poem recounts that journey.

     Heaven and Earth: The cosmological manifestations of *yin* and *yang*: Heaven as the active generative force of the Cosmos and Earth as the receptive generative force.

     quiet mystery: See *Key Terms*.

49   **Peach-Blossom Spring:** T'ao Ch'ien's classic poem-fable tells of a fisherman who discovers a secluded farming village at Peach-Blossom Spring, unknown to the outside world, where people live in peace and contentment, untroubled by the world's concerns.

51   **Meandering River:** See p. 30 and note. But here, the war has left the park and its fine houses in ruins.

     inner-pattern: See *Key Terms*.

52   **adoration:** An aesthetic appreciation or delight through which we come to the enlightenment of inner-pattern, a kind of rapturous aesthetic experience of the wild mountain realm as a single overwhelming whole.

53   **Li Po:** The great poet and friend of Tu Fu. Li Po had become involved, perhaps unwittingly, with the leader of a minor rebellion in the southeast. Once the rebellion had been put down, Li was banished to a waste region in the far southwest—an exile few survived.

spirit . . . dream: As described in the note to p. 46, it was popularly believed that spirits startle away when scared and drift far away during sleep. So long as the person is alive, the spirit is constricted in its movements. The spirit of a dead person, on the other hand, has complete freedom of movement, even over vast distances. It was also popularly thought that when someone enters dreams, it is that person's traveling spirit. Hence, Tu's worry.

54   **farmland fertility altars:** Chapter 46 of the *Tao Te Ching* says:

> When all beneath heaven abides in Way,
> fast horses are kept to work the fields.
> When all beneath heaven forgets Way,
> war horses are bred among the fertility altars.

57   Written in a commoner's voice, for which see note to p. 20.

61   **Thoughts:** This term (興, *hsing*) recurs in Tu Fu's titles and elsewhere, its full meaning being something like "what burgeons forth in consciousness." This is fundamentally different than the closest equivalent in English, "thoughts," because the sense of "burgeoning" reflects the Taoist/Ch'an generative cosmology operating within consciousness (as opposed to thought as a linear train of mental events).

64   *Ch'i*: See *Key Terms*.

68   **geese . . . news:** In classical Chinese poetry, migrating geese carry letters between separated loved ones.
    ill-used ghost: Ch'ü Yüan (343–278 BCE), China's first great identifiable poet. An admirable minister, he was exiled by a deluded ruler and eventually drowned himself in the Sun-Weave River, thus becoming the archetype of banished officials.

69   **original-nature:** In Ch'an, consciousness itself emptied of all contents.
    Emptiness empty: See *Key Terms*.

73   **Star River:** The Milky Way.

74 Written in a commoner's voice, for which see note to p. 20.
fulling-stones: Fulling cloth to make thick, warm clothes by pounding it on a stone was a grief-filled autumn ritual for women who would send the clothes to their husbands and sons who were far away at war and facing winter.

78 **occurrence appearing of itself:** *Tzu-jan* (自 然), literally "self-ablaze," from which comes "self-so" or "the of-itself," and a near synonym for *Tao.* But it is best translated as "occurrence appearing of itself," for it is meant to emphasize the particularity and self-sufficiency, the selfless and spontaneous *thusness,* of the ten thousand things in the ongoing transformation of Presence emerging from Absence. Like his great predecessors Tao Ch'ien and Hsieh Ling-yün, Tu spoke in a time of struggle and distraction of "returning to *tzu-jan.*"

79 **sparse:** See *Key Terms.*

80 **sun-carriage:** The sun was popularly imagined as a carriage driven by the great Sun-Mother and drawn by six dragons, all of which recur in Tu's poems.

81 **monkey sage:** Referring to the monkey trainer in *Chuang Tzu* 2.13:

> To wear yourself out illuminating the unity of all things without realizing that they're the same—this is called *three in the morning.* Why *three in the morning*? There was once a monkey trainer who said at feeding time, "You get three in the morning and four in the evening." The monkeys got very angry, so he said, "Okay, I'll give you four in the morning and three in the evening." At this, the monkeys were happy again. Nothing was lost in either name or reality, but they were angry one way and pleased the other. This is why the sage brings *yes this* and *no that* together and rests in heaven the equalizer. This is called taking two paths at once.

85 **spirit gone:** See notes to pp. 46 and 53.

92 *Ch'i*-**Siting:** Diviners who could feel the movement of *ch'i* through the landscape were hired to determine the best site for a house. For *ch'i,* see *Key Terms.*

on a whim . . . **Mountain-Shadow home:** See note to p. 15. Wang Hui-chih lived in Mountain-Shadow and took a small boat "on a whim" to visit his friend, then returned "on a whim" to his "mountain-shadow home."

94 **idle:** Idleness is the effortless and spontaneous movement of Way. To live in idleness was therefore a spiritual ideal widespread among the artist-intellectuals of ancient China, a kind of meditative wandering in which you move with that effortless spontaneity of Way (hence, *wu-wei*, for which see *Introduction*, p. 6), a practice that ideally defines everyday experience. Tu Fu says of this practice that "it is here, in idleness, I am real." Etymologically, the character for idleness connotes "profound serenity and quietness," its pictographic elements rendering a tree standing alone within the double gates to a courtyard: 閑. Or in its alternate form, a moon shining through open gates: 閒. See the *Introduction*, p. 5.

95 **Cut-Short Poem:** A standard poetic form that is half the size of the classic eight-line form, hence, "cut-short."

102 **fisher-cormorants:** The Chinese trained cormorants for fishing.

104 *Ch'in:* See note to p. 34.

105 **Kindred-Tree:** The *ch'in* (see note to p. 34) was made from the wood of kindred-trees, which gave the trees a certain spiritual aura.

106 **Yangtze . . . Star River:** China's Yangtze and Yellow Rivers were thought to flow east out to sea and then ascend to become the Star River (Milky Way), flow back across the sky, then descend into the far western mountains to become the headwaters of the two rivers.

109 **brocade land:** Altar-Whole was also known as Brocade City, as the area was once famous for the brocade produced there.

111 **sage of cap-strained wine:** T'ao Ch'ien, Tu Fu's great predecessor in the poetic tradition, lived in such poor reclusion that he strained homemade wine through his hat.

122 ***ch'an* stillness:** *Ch'an* is the Chinese translation of *dhyana*, Sanskrit for "sitting meditation." The Ch'an form of Buddhism takes that name because it focuses so resolutely on sitting meditation. See *Introduction*, p. 5 ff.

132 **9/9 Festival:** See note to p. 31.
Heaven and Earth: See note to p. 48.

134 **White-Crane:** The orchard where Buddha died, so named because upon his death the trees burst into white blossom and resembled white cranes.
Absence . . . Presence: See *Key Terms*.
transmits the lamp: In Ch'an Buddhism, this lamp is absolute insight, which is passed from teacher to student directly, outside of word and text, idea and institution. One of the major texts in Ch'an literature is the *Transmission of the Lamp*, which recounts enlightening stories from Ch'an's lineage of great teachers.
dwells nowhere: A fundamental aspect of Ch'an awakening, non-dwelling means inhabiting the movement of thought or life as part of Tao's great transformation, rather than clinging to a permanent self: a stable and enduring center of identity that sustains itself in turn by clinging to a constellation of assumptions and ideas. See also p. 136.

142 **quiet mystery:** See *Key Terms*.

150 **watch:** There were five watches in the night, two hours each, beginning at 7 p.m. and ending at 5 a.m. The night-watch also served a military purpose: an announcement from the guard that all was well. Tu Fu frequently used it as an image pointing to the dire social situation.

152 **dry throat:** Tu Fu was constantly thirsty because of his illnesses, as he mentions in the poem on p. 153.
inner-pattern: See *Key Terms*.

154 **Chang Hsü:** One of the greatest calligraphers in the Chinese tradition, Chang Hsü (c. 675–759 CE) was especially famous for his wild-cursive calligraphy. He was a serious Ch'an practitioner and often drank wine, the combination of which liberated him to scrawl out calligraphy with the selfless and spontaneous energy of the Cosmos, described by ancient Chinese as *wu-wei* (see *Introduction*, p. 6). Chang was a friend of Tu Fu's, and in an early poem Tu describes him as a "sage of cursive-script," saying how, after three cups of wine, he scatters paper sheets of calligraphy "like scraps of cloud and mist." Chang died in 759, about six years before this poem was written. Some of his wild-cursive script still survives, and is much celebrated.

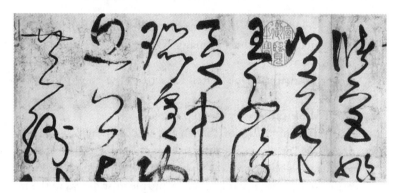

Chang Hsü (c. 675–759 CE): "Four Ancient-Style Poems" (detail)
Liaoning Provincial Museum, Shenyang.

two original masters: Chang Chih (2nd c. CE) and Wang Hsi-chih (4th c. CE).

155 **Solar-Origin Tree:** According to myth, the sun is ten crows, one for each day of the week. They perch in the huge Solar-Origin Tree in the east waiting for their turn to rise.
River-Source: In the cultural legend, the Yangtze River begins in the mythic Bright-Posterity Mountains in the West, at River-Source.

159 **geese . . . letters:** See note to p. 68.

160 **Lumen-Regal:** A legendary beauty of the Han Dynasty.

165 **Star River raft:** After flowing out to sea in the east, the Yangtze and Yellow Rivers were thought to ascend and rarify, becoming the Star River (Milky Way). This celestial river then crosses the sky and descends

in the far west to form the headwaters of the Yangtze and Yellow Rivers. The legend of the Star River raft tells of a Yangtze fisherman who one day saw a strange raft floating past his house. It was empty, so he climbed aboard, wondering where it might take him. The raft carried him downstream and eventually up into the Star River, where it became a star. The star drifted slowly back across the sky toward the west, and so came to be known as the Wandering Star. See also pp. 238 and 242.

167 **besiege-chess:** The Chinese invented the game of chess (see also p. 101), which existed there in many variants. Besiege-chess was one of those variants.

gongs and drums: One beaten for retreat, the other for advance.

168 **South Mountain:** See note to p. 31.

Lao Tzu: Seminal sage of Taoism and author of the *Tao Te Ching* (see *Introduction*, p. 4). According to legend, Lao Tzu was sick at heart over the ways of this world—so he left China, crossing Sheath-Ravine Pass into the west, accompanied by purple mist. It was in the pass, at the request of the border guard, that he wrote out his *Tao Te Ching*.

170 **Weaver-Girl:** The star Vega, on the shores of the Star River. According to legend, she wove the cloth of sky from its patterns of cloud. Eventually she married Herdboy (Altair), but the two were so entranced with each other that she neglected her weaving. Goddess Queen-Mother created the Star River to separate them, and sent Weaver-Girl back to her weaving. The couple thereafter lived on opposite shores of the Star River and were only allowed to meet one night of the year, on the seventh day of the seventh month, when magpies formed a bridge across the river.

171 **Fragrant field-rice . . . emperor-birds:** A particularly noteworthy example of how Tu Fu can dismantle grammar for poetic effect.

173 **Slumber-Dragon, Leap-Stallion:** Well-known figures from Chinese history, both of whom were associated with the Amble-Awe region. Slumber-Dragon was a great cultural hero, and Leap-Stallion an infamous villain.

174 **sun-carriage:** See note to p. 80.

175 **dark-enigma:** See *Key Terms*.

185 **summon my far-off spirit:** When someone died far from home, their family would perform a ritual to call their roaming spirit home for burial. See notes to pp. 46 and 53.

188 **fireflies . . . what you know:** It was popularly thought that the rhythms of firefly flashes could somehow predict the future.

200 **flame flickering . . . trouble:** If a lamp flame suddenly flickered out, it was traditionally considered a bad omen.

205 **North Mountain's bitter thorn-bean:** Referring to two ancient recluses who withdrew to North Mountain in protest during turbulent times and lived on thorn-beans until they finally died of cold and hunger.

208 **Dragon-Horse:** Dragon-Horse Temple, where the portraits of national heroes and great statesmen hung.

209 **no-mind:** Perhaps the concept most essential to Ch'an awakening, *no-mind* is synonymous with *empty-mind*: consciousness emptied of all contents. See also *Key Terms*: Mind.

220 **dharma:** In Ch'an Buddhism, *dharma* refers to the teachings of the Ch'an tradition. But Ch'an's essential teaching exists outside of words and ideas, which leads to *dharma*'s most fundamental meaning: the sheer thusness of things that is the true teaching, and also the texture of Tu Fu's poetry.

221 **Thoughts:** See note to p. 61.

222 **knotting ropes:** The Chinese *quipu*, a primitive linguistic and record-keeping system.

228 Great-Forge: Tao.

236 lost sage: Yang Chu, a shadowy proto-Taoist philosopher who once wept at a fork in the road because he knew either choice would only lead to another fork, with the result that he would become more and more lost.
drowned poet: Ch'ü Yüan, for which see note to p. 68.

238 Tu Fu's note: "I have just passed two miles beyond the lake's southern shore."
raft . . . Wander Star: See note to p. 165.
Southern Darkness: From *Chuang Tzu* 1.1:

> In Northern Darkness there lives a fish called Bright-Posterity. This Bright-Posterity is so huge that it stretches who knows how many thousand miles. When it changes into a bird it's called Two-Moon. This Two-Moon bird has a back spreading who knows how many thousand miles, and when it thunders up into flight its wings are like clouds hung clear across the sky. It churns up the sea and sets out on its migration to Southern Darkness, which is the Lake of Heaven.

239 floating-ant: Expensive wine was fermented in silver jars covered with cloth. During the fermentation process, a layer of scum formed on the surface of the wine. When this worthless layer was skimmed off and sold to those who could afford nothing better, it was called "floating-ant wine."

240 Seemingly written in some kind of quasi-mythic commoner's voice (cf. note to p. 20).
sea-goddess tear . . . pearl: It was popularly imagined that pearls were the tears of sea-goddesses.

243 Earth-Yellow . . . Provision-Sage: Emperors from the earliest mythic times, who created order and harmony on earth.

KEY TERMS

An Outline of Tu Fu's Conceptual World

Presence　有

The empirical universe, described in Taoist philosophy as the ten thousand things in constant transformation.

    Ref: 134, 147, 216, 239.

Absence　無

The pregnant emptiness from which the ever-changing realm of Presence perpetually arises. Not some kind of metaphysical realm, Absence is material reality seen as single a generative tissue: the ontological substrate infused mysteriously with a generative energy. Presence, then, is material reality seen differentiated into its ten thousand forms. Although made of the same material as Presence, Absence is "absence" or "emptiness" because it has no particular form. Because of its generative nature, it shapes itself into the individual forms of the Cosmos, then reshapes itself into other forms: the ten thousand things in the constant process of change. In fact, a more literal translation of Absence might be "formless," in contrast to "form-ful" for Presence. Absence is known directly in meditation (widely practiced by ancient Chinese poets and intellectuals), where it is experienced as empty consciousness itself, known in Ch'an terminology as "empty-mind" or "no-mind": the formless generative source of thoughts.

    Ref: 134, 147, 180, 216, 239.

Way (Tao)　道

The Tao of Taoism. The generative ontological process through which all things arise and pass away. As such, Tao might provisionally be divided into Presence and Absence. This is a prime example of overlapping terminology struggling to name the fundamental nature of reality—for in its actual usage, Tao is nearly identified with Absence, because however much Presence takes its various forms, it always remains part of the ongoing generative tissue of formless Absence.

See also *Introduction*, p. 4 ff.

Ref: 97, 142.

Empty/Emptiness 空 and 虛

A virtual synonym for Absence, and often used to describe mountain landscapes, empty-mind perception (of those landscapes), or consciousness emptied of all contents.

Ref: *passim*.

Sparse 微

The everyday meanings of 微 as "sparse/slight/small/subtle" are generally infused with philosophic resonance in poetry: things on the emergent side of the origin-moment in that cosmology of Tao's ongoing generative unfolding, just barely come into existence as differentiated entities or not quite vanished back into the undifferentiated ground.

Ref: 79, 88, 89, 101, 105, 120, 147, 154, 157, 158, 166, 195, 213, 218, 226, 227.

Quiet Mystery 幽

Appearing often in recluse poetry, 幽 always infuses the surface meaning "quiet solitude" with rich philosophical depths, beginning with the sense of "dark/secret/hidden/mystery." And that leads finally to the term's deepest level, where it forms a terminological pair with 微 ("sparse"). Here it means forms, the ten thousand things, on the not-yet-emergent side of the origin-moment: just as they are about to emerge from the formless ground of Absence, or just after they vanish back into that ground.

Ref: 15, 30, 48, 49, 92, 95, 101, 122, 134, 142, 186, 221.

Loom of Origins 機

A mythological description of Tao's generative process, the Cosmos in constant transformation. Chuang Tzu, the seminal Taoist writer, describes that ontology/cosmology like this: "The ten thousand things all emerge from a loom of origins, and they all vanish back into it."

Ref: 75, 170.

Dark-Enigma 玄

Another example of concepts blurring at foundational levels, *dark-enigma* is functionally equivalent to Absence—the generative, ontological tissue from which the ten thousand things spring—but Absence before it is named. For once we name it, we have entered the realm of the differentiated and therefore lost it. Or more properly, dark-enigma is Way before it is named, before the concepts of Absence and Presence give birth to one another: existence without names and concepts, as it is in and of itself, the formless generative tissue where consciousness and the empirical Cosmos share their source.

Ref: 175, 223.

Inner-Pattern 理

The philosophical meaning of *inner-pattern,* which originally referred to the veins and markings in a precious piece of jade, is something akin to what we might call natural law. It is the system of principles or patterns that governs the unfolding of Tao as it unfurls into the ten thousand things. Inner-pattern therefore weaves Absence and Presence into a single boundless tissue.

Ref: 34, 51, 78, 88, 152, 205.

Ch'i 氣

氣 is often described as the universal life-force breathing through things. But this presumes a dualism that separates reality into matter and a breath-force (spirit) that infuses it with life. Like the Absence/Presence dichotomy, that dualism may be useful as an approach to understanding, but more fully understood, *ch'i* is actually both breath-force and matter simultaneously. It is a single tissue generative through and through, the matter and energy of the Cosmos seen together as a single breath-force surging though its perpetual transformations.

Ref: *passim.*

Mind   心

心 sometimes means "mind" in the conventional English sense of the word, as the center of language and thought and memory, the mental apparatus of identity. But generally in poetry and Ch'an, *mind* refers to consciousness emptied of all contents, a state reached through deep meditation (also confusingly known as "empty-mind" or "no-mind" to distinguish it from "mind" in its conventional sense.) This empty-mind is nothing other than Absence, that generative cosmological tissue—for it is the empty source of thought and memory, and also an empty mirror open via perception to the ten thousand things (Presence).

In ancient China, there was no fundamental distinction between heart and mind: 心 connotes all that we think of in the two concepts together. In fact, the ideogram is a stylized version of the earlier 忄, which is an image of the heart muscle with its chambers at the locus of veins and arteries.

Ref: *passim.*

Ch'i-Mind/Thought   意

Containing the pictographic element for "mind" (心), 意 has a range of meanings: "intentionality/desire/meaning/insight/thought/intelligence/mind as the faculty of thought." The natural Western assumption would be that these meanings refer to human consciousness, but 意 is also often used philosophically in describing the non-human world, as the "intentionality/desire/intelligence" that shapes the ongoing cosmological process of change and transformation. Each particular thing, at its very origin, has its own 意, as does the Cosmos as a whole. 意 can therefore be described as the "intentionality/intelligence/desire" infusing Absence (or Tao) and shaping its burgeoning forth into Presence, the ten thousand things of this Cosmos. It could also be described as the "intentionality," the inherent ordering capacity, shaping the creative force of *ch'i.*

This range of meaning links human intention/thought to the originary movements of the Cosmos. And that link explains this translation's use of the term "*ch'i*-mind," which is meant to open the cosmological context for the idea of an "intelligence" that infuses all existence, and of which human thought is but one manifestation. So, 意 is a capacity that human thought and emotion share with wild landscape and, indeed, the entire Cosmos, a reflection of the Chinese assumption that the human and non-human form a single tissue that "thinks" and "wants." Hence, thought/identity is not a transcendental spirit-realm separate from and looking out on reality, as we assume in the West. Instead, it is woven wholly into the ever-generative *ch'i*-tissue—which is to say, it is woven wholly into a living, "intelligent" Cosmos.

Ref: 117, 133, 135, 144, 172, 177, 178, 192, 227–28, 236.

Eye/Sight/Looking 目, 眼, 見, 直, etc.

Once mind is emptied of all content through meditation, the act of perception becomes a spiritual act: empty-mind mirroring the world, making inside outside and outside inside. This is the heart of Ch'an as a landscape practice that shapes the imagistic texture of Chinese poetry. In such mirror-deep perception, earth's rivers-and-mountains landscape replaces thought and even identity itself, revealing the unity of consciousness and landscape/ Cosmos that is the heart of sage dwelling for artist-intellectuals like Tu Fu.

Ref: *passim.*

FINDING LIST

1. Owen, Stephen. *The Poetry of Tu Fu* (poem number). Complete scholarly translation, bilingual. Owen's poem numbers correspond to the fascicle and poem number within fascicle in the most widely available and thorough scholarly edition in Chinese: *Tu Shih Hsiang Chu* 杜詩詳注 by Ch'iu Chao-ao 仇兆鰲. Owen also includes cross-references to many other editions.

2. Yang, Lun 楊倫. *Tu Shih Ching Ch'üan* 杜詩鏡銓 (fascicle and page number). Fascicles are consistent in all editions, though page numbers for poems may differ slightly within fascicles.

PAGE	1. *The Poetry of Tu Fu*	2. *Tu Shih Ching Ch'üan*
13	1.2	1.1a
14	1.1	1.2a
15	1.4	1.2a
16	1.6	1.2b
17	1.8	1.3a
18	2.13	1.21a
20	2.14	2.3b
29	2.11	1.25a
30	3.43	2.29b
31	3.25	2.23a
32	3.30	2.24b
33	4.6	3.8a
39	4.20	3.17b
40	4.18	3.18b

DAVID HINTON's original *Tu Fu* was the first full-length verse translation of Tu Fu published in America. It was his first book, and since then his many translations of ancient Chinese poetry and philosophy have earned wide acclaim for creating compelling contemporary works that convey the actual texture and density of the originals. The author also of singular books of essays and poetry, Hinton has been awarded a Guggenheim Fellowship, numerous fellowships from N.E.A. and N.E.H, both major awards given for poetry translation in the United States, and a lifetime achievement award by the American Academy of Arts and Letters.